HERSTORY

The Legal History of Chinese American Women

Chang C. Chen, PhD, JD

Edited : Herman Chan

Copyright © 2016 by Chang C. Chen

All Rights Reserved

No part of this book may be reproduced or utilized in any form or by any means, electronic or mechanical, or by any information storage or retrieval system, without written permission from the publisher.

ISBN-13: 978-1539118954
ISBN-10: 1539118959
LCCN: 2017900089

HERSTORY

The Legal History of Chinese American Women

Chang C. Chen, PhD, JD

Edited : Herman Chan

Includes bibliographical references.

FOREWORD

While Dr. Chang C. Chen has authored more than 50 books in Chinese, whose topics range from law to marriage, "**Herstory**-the Legal History of Chinese American Women" is her first book in English. It is also her most significant book to date. Even though it took her three painstaking years to research, in actuality, Dr Chen has been preparing for this book her whole life.

Dr. Chen grew up in Taiwan and immigrated to America 44 years ago to pursue her graduate studies. After obtaining her Ph.D in biochemistry from Rutgers University and J. D. from Columbia University Law School, she launched an illustrious legal career spanning 25 years. One of her most notorious and victorious lawsuits was a pro bono case where she negotiated against the banks on behalf of 250 Taiwan families who had purchased Lehman Brothers junk bonds. The Taiwan Bar Association then prosecuted her for her good deed which they alleged to be "illegal practice of Taiwan law." Dr. Chen prevailed in both the Taiwan District Court and the Appellate Court.

Not one to just practice law, she was elected to be a Taiwan Senator and even hosted four television shows. During the 1990's her most popular program "Chang C. Chen Talking Law" on Star-TV in Hong Kong catapulted her into the limelight. She swiftly became a celebrity female attorney and personality, still to this day a rare feat in Taiwan.

This book is a culmination of the **Herstory** Exhibition she curated. What started as a small personal project for Dr. Chen snowballed into a global sensation. International libraries, museums around the globe from Taiwan, Los Angeles, San Francisco, Hawaii, New York & more have showcased Herstory. When she started this project, a search in the index of the Library of Congress for the phrase "Chinese American Women" yielded not a single result. Now, thanks to **Herstory**, thousands and thousands of entries exist. Dr. Chen is humbled, due to her efforts, Chinese American Women have secured their place in history.

Herman Chan
Co-curator of Herstory exhibition

PREFACE

By the time 2012 arrived, I had been a lawyer for over 25 years and a Chinese American for 40 years, and I was overcome by a strong sense of duty to pen this book, "The Legal History of Chinese Americans- Battle between the Dragon and the Eagle". From the start, I wrote it as a mission to share my personal experiences and research. I never expected more than a few readers, after all, a laundry list of legal cases is not exactly sexy reading. But I could not imagine that it would only take one reader to change my life forever. That reader is Dr. Yu-Tung Chang, Executive Director of the National History Museum in Taiwan. He encouraged me to curate an exhibition based on the legal history of Chinese American women.

I have been many things in my life, but I have never been a curator. Trusting Dr. Yu-Tung Chang's belief in me, I naively drove straight in. With benefit of hindsight, I can say now that my curating experience proved the Chinese proverb "Seeking no excess finds you noble" erroneous. I had to literally beg people day and night to help out everyday for everything. Some said no, but to my surprise many said yes. Inspired by such kindness, I knew I was on the right path and that I needed to do the right thing for all these people who put their faith in me to bring the stories of their lives and of their ancestors to life. All of my groveling for favors was worth it.

Entitled "**Herstory**—the Legal History of Chinese American Women," in May 2015, Herstory was officially unveiled to the public at the National History Museum in Taiwan, Tainan Historical Meeting Hall and Chung Hua Art Museum.

In 2016, **Herstory** exhibition opened at the San Francisco Main Library, Taipei Economic and Cultural Office in New York, the New York Public Library Chatham Square Branch, the Chicago Public Library Chinatown Branch and the San Mateo County Library in Foster City.

In 2017, **Herstory** will travel to the Los Angeles Central Library, UC Berkeley Ethnic Studies Library and Hawaii State Library. The response has been overwhelming and I am deeply grateful for all the assistance I receive everywhere and from everyone.

The entire contents of this book are derived from the cases of the U.S. Supreme Court and the Supreme Courts of various states, specifically, cases fought by the Chinese American women who disproved the ancient Chinese teaching of "Only unpleasant endings emerge from lawsuits".

Starting in 1852, the cases document women who fought for basic legal standing, for equal treatment in the eyes of the law and for citizenship and immigration rights. One case from 1874 from San Francisco describes a group of recent immigrants who were set to be deported because they were labeled as "lewd and immoral" merely due to their style of dress. The women took this injustice to court and the U.S. Supreme Court ruled in their favor, stating that the California laws were in conflict with federal immigrations laws and the women were released. In another San Francisco case from 1885, the California State Supreme Court ruled that Chinese American children had a right to public education and to attend public schools because of Tape v. Hurley, 66 Cal.473(1885)'s case.

This book is about the ordinary people who fought for their rights and in doing so helped shape a new world for all Chinese Americans.

Chang C. Chen 邱龍
2016

Herstory exhibition has travelled to the following museums and libraries:

National Museum of History, Taiwan
6/19 - 8/2, 2015

Tainan Historical Public Meeting Hall, Taiwan
9/25 - 11/8, 2015

Changhwa Art Museum, Taiwan
11/24 - 12/12, 2015

San Francisco Main Library
3/19 - 7/14, 2016

New York Taipei Economic and Cultural Center
4/1 - 4/30, 2016

New York Public Library Chatham Square Branch
9/28 - 10/30, 2016

Foster City Public Library
8/20 - 9/30, 2016

Chicago Public Library Chinatown Branch
9/1 - 10/31, 2016

Los Angeles Central Library
11/1, 2016 - 2/26, 2017

Hawaii State Library
3/1 - 4/30, 2017

More to come.......

For my sons

Jason Tser-Seng Chen & Greg Tser-Ming Chen

INDEX

1852	Ah Toy's lawsuit was dismissed due to the ruling in People v. Hall in 1852.	10
1868	Burlingame Treaty was the first equal treaty between the U.S. and China.	12
1874	In Chu Lung v. Freeman 92 U.S. 275 (1874), twenty-two Chinese women fought for their dignity.	14
1882	The Chinese Exclusion Act was signed into law by President Chester A. Arthur in 1882.	16
1885	In Tape v. Hurley, 66 Cal. 473 (1885), Mamie Tape fought for the right to public education.	18
1896	Polly Bemis became a legendary Chinese-American pioneer.	20
1898	In United States v. Wong Kim Ark, 169 U.S. 649 (1898), the Court ruled that practically everyone born in the United States is a U.S. citizen.	24
1909	Bow Kum's murder led to the Chinatown gang war.	26
1909	The Angry Angel of Chinatown, Donaldina Cameron, rescued 3000 Chinese slave girls.	28
1912	Tye Leung Schulze became the first Chinese-American woman to vote in the presidential primary.	30
1916	Quok Shee was the longest involuntary resident of Angel Island.	32
1922	The Cable Act of 1922 forbade Chinese men from marrying white women.	36
1927	Martha Lum was denied entry to the public school for white children. *Gong Lum v. Rice, 275 U.S. 78 (1927)*	38
1943	The 1943 Treaty was for the relinquishment of extraterritorial rights in China.	40
1943	The Magnuson Act of 1950 encouraged Chinese to serve in the U.S. military in exchange for citizenship.	42
1943	Chinese American women proudly served in the U.S. military.	44
1945	Stories of three Amerasians	52
1953	Eileen Chang became U.S. citizen under the Refugee Relief Act of 1953.	58

1964	Civil Rights Act was passed in 1964.	60
1965	The Immigration and Nationality Act of 1965 changed the face of the American population.	62
1967	Freedom to marry was upheld in Loving v. Virginia, 388 U.S. 1 (1967).	64
1974	Lau v. Nichols, 414 U.S. 563 (1974) helped shape the bilingual education system.	66
1977	Mi Chu won her employment with the Library of Congress under the Equal Employment Opportunity Act of 1972.	68
1979	Patricia Cowett was the first Chinese-American judge.	70
1982	Vincent Chin's murder was a hate-crime.	72
1983	Lily Lee Chen became the first Chinese American woman mayor.	74
1993	Sister Ping smuggled all the villagers from Shengmei, Fujian Province to America.	76
2000	Florence Fang became owner of a mainstream newspaper-the San Francisco Examiner.	78
2001	Elaine Chao was the first Chinese-American woman cabinet secretary.	80
2009	Dolly Gee became the first female Chinese-American federal judge.	81
2009	Judy Chu was the first Chinese-American Congresswoman.	81
2009	California Governor Schwarzenegger apologized for the historical Chinese exclusion laws.	82
2011	The Senate apologized for all the Chinese exclusion laws.	84
2012	Congress apologized for the Chinese Exclusion Act.	86
2012	Residents in Riverside California saved Chinatown history.	88
	Acknowledgments	90
	Photo Credits	91

1852

Ah Toy's lawsuit was dismissed due to the ruling in People v. Hall in 1852.

The most notorious Chinese-American prostitute, Ah Toy, sued Yee Ah Tye for demanding that her Dupont Street prostitutes pay him a tax. In the 1854 case of People v. Hall, 4 Cal.399, the judge ruled that the Chinese had no business in American courts, and could not testify nor become witnesses. Ah Toy's lawsuit was ultimately dismissed.

1852年，當時最出名的華人老鴇阿彩（Ah Toy）告幫派份子余大（Yee Ah Tye）勒索，但因1854年豪爾案（People of the State of California v. George W. Hall, 4 Cal.399）判決華人無權在法院做證，阿彩的訴訟也泡湯了。

阿彩是當時舊金山的傳奇人物，1848年就到美國執壺，她的營業所門口經常排著長龍，警察偶爾還得拔槍維持秩序。她後來嫁給一位富商，活到99歲。

---

1. https://en.wikipedia.org/wiki/Ah_Toy

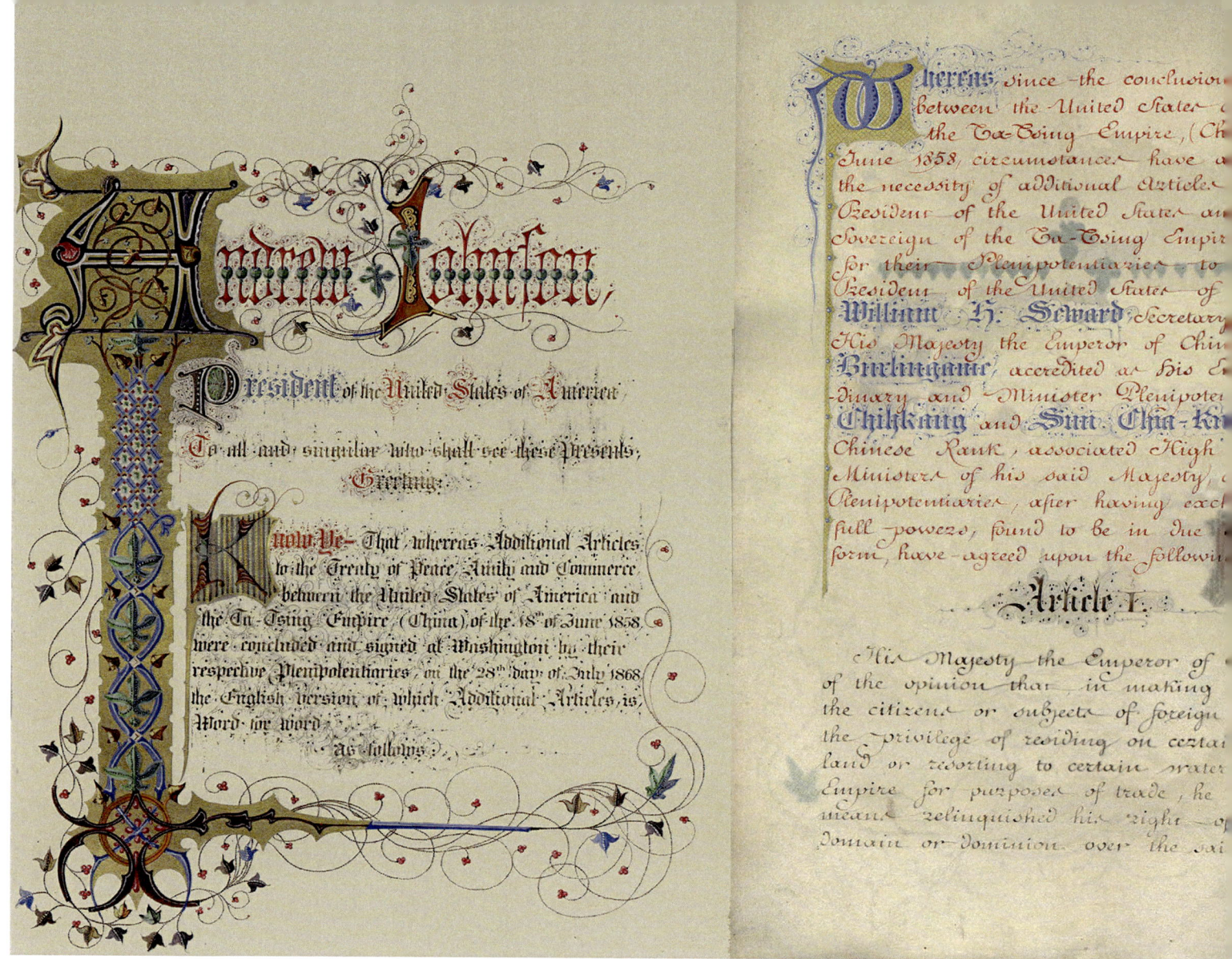

1868

Burlingame Treaty was the first equal treaty between the U.S. and China.

Granting China most favored nation status, the Burlingame-Seward Treaty formally established friendly ties between China and the United States. The Treaty advocated equal treatment of China and a welcoming stance toward Chinese immigrants.

This Treaty also opened the door for Chinese laborers to immigrate to the U.S. During economic depression, white laborers blamed cheap Chinese laborers for their unemployment. Congress amended The Burlingame Treaty and in its place, The Chinese Exclusion Act was passed in 1882.

「蒲安臣條約」又稱「中美天津條約續增條約」，是1868年清朝與美國簽訂的第一個平等條約。在該條約中，美國給與中國最惠國待遇。「蒲安臣條約」的簽訂使得美國成為中國派遣留學生的首選國。1872年，第一批中國幼童乘船前往美國，從此掀開了中國公派留學生前往美國學習的第一頁。

此條約也為中國勞工移民美國敞開了大門。不過由於經濟不景氣，美國國內對華工激烈排斥，美國國會在1880年修改了「蒲安臣條約」，又在1882年通過了「排華法案」。

---

2. http://immigrants.harpweek.com/ChineseAmericans/2KeyIssues/BurlingameTreaty1868.htm
3. https://en.wikipedia.org/wiki/Burlingame_Treaty

#	Names	Age		#	Name	Age
1	Ah Sop	20		16	Ah Of	17
2	Ah Fung	20		17	Yun Hea	17
3	Ah Foo	22		18	Ah Duck	20
4	Hee Choi	13		19	Ah Kum	17
5	Dy Kum	17		20	Hong Choi	20
6	Choi Fong	19		21	Chun Lo	22
7	Sing Choi	19		22	Dy Hea	16
8	Ah Sin	19				
9	Sow Yung	20				
10	Soni Hee	21				
11	Tsun Jow	21				
12	Ah Fon	25				
13	Ah Hui	15				
14	Lung Choi	20				
15	Ah Kee	15				

The names of the 22 Chinese women in the Supreme Court files（1874）

1874

In Chu Lung v. Freeman 92 U.S. 275 (1874), twenty-two Chinese women fought for their dignity.

In Chu Lung v. Freeman, 92 U.S. 275, Chu Lung and 21 other Chinese women who arrived in San Francisco were classified as "lewd and debauched" and, therefore, must be prostitutes. Upon hearing testimony from a witness that only lewd Chinese women wore colorful bellybands, the judge found all 22 women guilty. However, the Supreme Court sided with the women. It ruled that Congress, not the states, had the power to regulate immigration. It declared that California law requiring a bond for all ill-defined class of people overstepped its boundary and that the women should be released.

1874年，22位華人女性從香港坐船到舊金山，移民官認為她們是來賣淫，因此拒絕她們入境。這些女性找了律師，在法庭與美國政府激辯聯邦的權利、州的權利以及婦女的權利。

一位傳教士作證說，淫蕩的中國女性都穿著大紅大綠的內衣。法官發現這些女性在衣袖裡果然都穿著花色鮮艷的內衣，因此判定她都是妓女。22位女性不服，上訴到聯邦巡迴法院，這次她們贏了。美國政府立刻上訴到最高法院。1878年3月最高法院的判決出爐，22位女性勝訴並立即被釋放。大法官米勒說：移民官不得有任意給人貼標籤及歧視的權力。這是華人女性在美國最高法院的第一個案例。

---

4. http://en.wikipedia.org/wiki/Page_Act_of_1875
5. Abrams, Kerry, "Polygamy, Prostitution, and the Federalization of Immigration Law," Colombia Law Review 105.3 (Apr. 2005).
6. George Anthony Peffer, "Forbidden Families: Emigration Experiences of Chinese Women Under the Page Law, 1875-1882," Journal of American Ethnic History 6.1 (Fall 1986).
7. Eithne Luibheid, Entry Denied: Controlling Sexuality at the Border (University of Minnesota Press, 2002)

1882

The Chinese Exclusion Act was signed into law by President Chester A. Arthur in 1882.

It was one of the most significant restrictions on free immigration in the U.S. history, prohibiting all immigration of Chinese laborers. The act followed the Angell Treaty of 1880, a set of revisions to the U.S.- China Burlingame Treaty of 1868 that allowed the U.S. to suspend Chinese immigration.

The Act was initially intended to last for ten years, but was renewed in 1892 with the Geary Act becoming permanent in 1902. The Chinese Exclusion Act was the first law implemented to prevent a specific ethnic group from immigrating to the United States. It was repealed by the Magnuson Act of 1943.

「排華法案」的內容為：
1. 停止華工及其眷屬入境十年。
2. 不准境內華人歸化為美國公民。
3. 華人一旦回中國探親，就不能再回美國。
4. 州法院和聯邦法院不得允許華人歸化為美國公民。

在「排華法案」於1892年即將到期前，國會再通過「吉爾里法案」將「排華法案」延長十年。直到1943年，中國成為美國第二次世界大戰的盟友，「排華法案」才被廢除。

8. https://en.wikipedia.org/wiki/Chinese_Exclusion_Act

1885

In Tape v. Hurley, 66 Cal. 473(1885), Mamie Tape fought for the right to public education.

Tape v. Hurley, 66 Cal. 473 (1885) was a landmark case in the California Supreme Court. In 1884, Mamie, then eight years old, was denied admission to the Spring Valley School due to her Chinese ancestry. Her parents sued the San Francisco Board of Education and won. Their argument was that the school violated California Political Code. The California Supreme Court upheld the decision. Justice McGuire wrote, "To deny a child, born of Chinese parents in this state, entrance to the public schools would be a violation of the law of the state and the Constitution of the United States."

A bill was quickly passed to establish the Oriental Public School in San Francisco. The school was renamed Gordon J. Lau Elementary School in 1998.

1848年以來，加州掀起淘金熱，短短一年就30萬人擠到加州，因為激增的人口，政府設立了7所公立學校。1852年，舊金山已有兩萬華人居民。1884年，出身富裕的華裔女孩 Mamie Tape 時年8歲，父母打算讓她就讀公立小學卻被拒收，因為當時的公立小學只收白人。

她的父母一狀告到加州最高法院，獲得勝訴。但舊金山教育委員會說服加州州議會，通過設置華裔專校的法案，讓華裔只能就讀華裔小學，堅決貫徹種族隔離政策。舊金山也因此在1859年成立第一所華人小學「東方公立小學」。此校經過多次更名，現為「劉貴明小學」，紀念這位人權鬥士。

---

9. https://en.wikipedia.org/wiki/Tape_v._Hurley
10. http://www.gilderlehrman.org/history-by-era/immigration-and-migration/timeline-terms/mamie-tape

1896

Polly Bemis became a legendary Chinese-American pioneer.

Polly Bemis was sold by her peasant father for two bags of much-needed seed. She was smuggled into the United States in 1872 and sold as a slave in San Francisco. In 1894, she married Charles Bemis to prevent herself from being deported.

She later gained her residence paper because she was able to prove that she could not apply in time due to a major snowstorm in Idaho in 1895.

Her cabin, known as Polly Bemis House, became a museum and was placed on the National Register of Historical Places in 1988. Her story was fictionalized in the 1991 film: A Thousand Pieces of Gold.

蒙古裔的Polly Bemis生在廣東，她被父親以兩袋種子的代價賣掉，又被轉賣到美國，最後在愛德荷州沃倫的地方定居。她任勞任怨、堅忍不拔，不但救了她先生的性命，也贏得了當地居民的友誼。

「吉爾里法案」通過後，1895年Polly Bemis和其他50名住在愛德荷的中國人，因為沒有居留權而將被驅逐出境，還好Polly Bemis證明當時當地下了一場大雪，交通中斷，迫使他們無法出門辦居留手續，Polly Bemis因禍得福，於1896年獲得美國永久居留權。

Polly Bemis是荒涼的愛達荷中部最早的墾荒者之一，她所居住的小木屋現已成為國家級的史蹟。她於1933年過世，享年80歲。她的生平被拍成電影「千金」。在父親眼中只值兩袋種子的Polly Bemis，在美國邊疆綻放出璀璨的花朵，傳播慈愛、溫柔、不屈的女性傳統美德，是美國華人女性的不朽傳奇。

---

11. https://en.wikipedia.org/wiki/Polly_Bemis
12. http://www.encyclopedia.com/doc/1G2-3446400031.html

In the District Court of the United States, for the District of Idaho.

THE UNITED STATES.

VS.

Polly Bemis

INFORMATION.
Violation Section 6, Act November 3rd, 1893.

UNITED STATES OF AMERICA, } ss.
DISTRICT OF IDAHO.

Be It Remembered, That James H. Forney, the Attorney of the United States for the District of Idaho, who prosecutes in behalf and with the authority of the United States, comes here in person into Court at this the October Term thereof, and for the United States gives the Court to understand and be informed that one *Polly Bemis* is a Chinese Laborer now residing in the State and District of Idaho, and has been such a resident for more than three years last past and within the jurisdiction of this Court, and that the said *Polly Bemis*, said Chinese laborer as aforesaid, failed and refused to comply with the provisions of the Act of Congress approved May the 5th, 1892, as amended by the Act of November the 3rd, 1893, in this: That the said *Polly Bemis* did not apply to the Collector of Internal Revenue of this District, or any other District, for a Certificate of Residence, and that the time for making said application has expired—Contrary to the form of the Statutes in such cases made and provided, and against the peace and dignity of the United States of America.

Wherefore, the said United States Attorney for the District of Idaho prays the consideration of the Court in the premises, and that due process of law may be awarded against the said *Polly Bemis*, defendant, in this behalf, to make him answer to the United States touching and concerning the premises.

Dated at Moscow, Idaho, this 13th day of Oct, 1895.

United States Attorney.

District of Idaho.—ss:

JAMES H. FORNEY, being duly sworn, says that he is the attorney for the United States for the District of Idaho; that he has read the foregoing information, knows the contents thereof, and that he believes it to be true.

1898

In United States v. Wong Kim Ark, 169 U.S. 649 (1898), the Court ruled that practically everyone born in the United States is a U.S. citizen.

Wong Kim Ark, who was born in San Francisco to Chinese parents around 1871, was denied re-entry to the United States after a trip abroad in 1894. He challenged the government's refusal to recognize his citizenship. The Supreme Court ruled in his favor, holding that the citizenship language in the Fourteenth Amendment encompassed essentially everyone born in the U.S.—even the U.S.-born children of foreigners—and could not be limited in its effect by an act of Congress.

黃金德（Wong Kim Ark）生於美國舊金山，父母都是美國合法居民。黃金德1890年回中國，再返美時，海關認定他是美國公民而允許他入境。1894年，黃金德再次前往中國，1895年返美時，卻因排華法案而被拒絕入境，黃金德乃提起訴訟。

1897年，在United States v. Wong Kim Ark, 169 U.S. 649 (1898) 一案中, 最高法院大法官認定：所有在美國出生的華人後裔，其父母非中國外交官員或公職人員，且在美國擁有永久住所者，在出生時即為美國公民。黃金德打贏這場官司後，他的三個兒子也都拿到公民權。「在美國出生，即為美國公民」的法理，掀起外國孕婦前往美國生產的「生育旅遊」潮。

Grand daughter (left) and great granddaughter (middle) of Wong Kim Ark and Dr. Chang C. Chen (right).

黃金德的孫女(左一)與曾孫女(中)與作者合影

---

13. United States v. Wong Kim Ark, 169 U.S. 649 (1898)
14. http://en.wikipedia.org/wiki/United_States_v._Wong_Kim_Ark

ACQUIT CHINAMEN OF KILLING BOW KUM

The Accused Make Low Bows of Gratitude to the Jury That Freed Them.

FOUR BROTHERS JUBILANT

Oriental Society Takes the Liberated Men to Pell Street for a Celebration.

There was great rejoicing among the members of the Four Brothers in Chinatown last night when news came from the Criminal Branch of the Supreme Court that Lau Tang and Lau Shong had been acquitted of the murder of little

The New York Times reported the acquittal of Bow Kum's killers.

The New York Times reported Bow Kum's murder on August 16, 1909.

YOUNG CHINESE GIRL SLAIN IN CHINATOWN

Stabbed Three Times and Hand of Her Husband Fits Bloody Print—He Is Arrested.

SAYS ANOTHER DID IT

Chin Len's Conflicting Stories and Circumstantial Evidence Convince the Police—Others Arrested Set Free.

1909

Bow Kum's murder led to the Chinatown gang war.

Born to a poor family in Guangdong, Bow Kum was sold by her parents for $40 and later bought by Lau He Dong, a member of the Snakehead gang in San Francisco, for $3,000.

Lau fell in love with her, but Bow Kum chose to marry a gardener and ran away with him to New York. Lau's love quickly turned to hate and he asked his gang to seek revenge. On August 15, 1909, Bow Kum was brutally murdered. Her husband was also part of a Chinese gang and they fought back. The war between the Chinatown gangs lasted more than a year. On January 11, 1910, the alleged killers, Lau He Dong and Lau Shong, were acquitted because each of their gangs produced contradictory evidence, and the jury could not decide who the real killers were.

The U.S. and the Chinese government brokered talks between the rival gangs at the end of 1910. New York's Chinatown eventually regained its peace in 1913.

甘苞（Bow Kum）是廣東窮人家的女兒，被父母以40美元的代價賣給人蛇，隨後又被以3,000美元的高價，轉賣給舊金山幫派頭目劉喜東。劉喜東很快就愛上了美艷的甘苞，只是甘苞愛的是林姓園丁，並跟他私奔到紐約。劉喜東向紐約的協勝堂求援，協勝堂要求林姓園丁所屬的安良堂還錢或還人，但遭到拒絕。

1909年8月15日，兩個殺手潛入甘苞家中將她謀殺。消息震驚了全紐約，一場血腥的幫派大戰就此展開。1910年1月，兇手被陪審團判無罪，因為兩派證人對兇手當時的行蹤供詞不一，陪審團因此無法將兇手定罪。1910年底，美國及中國政府正式出面，安排安良堂及協勝堂簽署停火協議，直到1913年，紐約中國城才恢復過往的繁榮。

---

15. https://en.wikipedia.org/wiki/Bow_Kum

1909

The Angry Angel of Chinatown, Donaldina Cameron, rescued 3000 Chinese slave girls.

Donaldina Cameron (July 26, 1869-January 4, 1968) was a Presbyterian missionary who advocated for social justice. She rescued and educated more than 3000 Chinese immigrant girls and women who were sold into slavery during her ministry from 1895 to 1934. Cameron House still stands today in San Francisco.

金美倫（Donaldina Cameron）被稱為「中國城的憤怒天使」，她是位白人傳教士，於1895年服務於舊金山中國城的「東方傳道少女之家」。她痛恨人蛇集團對中國女孩的凌虐，經常伴著警察、帶著斧頭，把這群被迫賣淫的中國女孩子從地板下、牆壁中救出來。在她主持「東方傳道少女之家」的40年間，救出了至少3,000位華裔小女孩。金美倫被這些小女孩尊稱為「老母」，但人口販子稱她為「白鬼」。「東方傳道少女之家」在1942年改名為「金美倫堂」，位於舊金山沙加緬度街920號，是有名的歷史地標。

---

16. Empheral New York, June 26, 2009 http://ephemeralnewyork.wordpress.com/tag/bow-kum/
17. http://www.foundsf.org/
18. http://en.wikipedia.org/wiki/Donaldina_Cameron
19. Chinatown's Angry Angel: The Story of Donaldina Cameron by Mildred Crowl Martin, May 1989
20. The New York Times, January 11,1910
21. The New York Times, January 16,1910
22. Mobsters in America, by Joseph Bruno,"Mobsters,Gangs,Crooks, and Other Creeps-Volume1, New York City",2011 http://ezinearticles.com/?Mobsters-in-America---The-Viious-Killing-of-Bow-Kum-Started-the-Tong-Wars-in-NY-Citys-Chinatown&id=5594717

1912

Tye Leung Schulze became the first Chinese-American woman to vote in the presidential primary.

Tye Leung was born in San Francisco in 1887. When she was 14, her parents arranged for her to marry an older man. She ran away and sought refuge with Donaldina Cameron. She became the first Chinese-American woman to pass the civil service examination. Not only was she the first Chinese woman hired to work at Angel Island, but she also became the first Chinese-American woman to vote in a presidential primary election when she cast a ballot in San Francisco on May 19, 1912.

梁亞娣（Tye Leung Schulze）在1887年生於舊金山。她14歲時，父母就安排她嫁給一個年長的男士。梁亞娣勇敢的離家去找金美倫傳教士學英文、研究基督教，後來成為第一位通過美國政府文官考試的華人女性。1912年的美國總統初選，梁亞娣是第一位有資格投票選舉的華人女性，而全美國女性到8年後才有投票權。舊金山紀事報說：梁亞娣投票選總統，是女性完全解放的現代運動。梁亞娣因為嫁給白人，不得不辭去合法的政府工作，但她繼續為舊金山華人提供翻譯及社會服務，深受華人尊重。她於85歲時辭世。梁亞娣一直勇敢的反抗任何加諸於她身上的限制，創造屬於自己的榮譽、尊嚴。她從未參加任何全國性的組織，也沒有任何法案以她命名。她的傳奇來自於她一生全心全意的投入反抗人類的偏見與固執。

---

23. https://en.wikipedia.org/wiki/Tye_Leung_Schulze

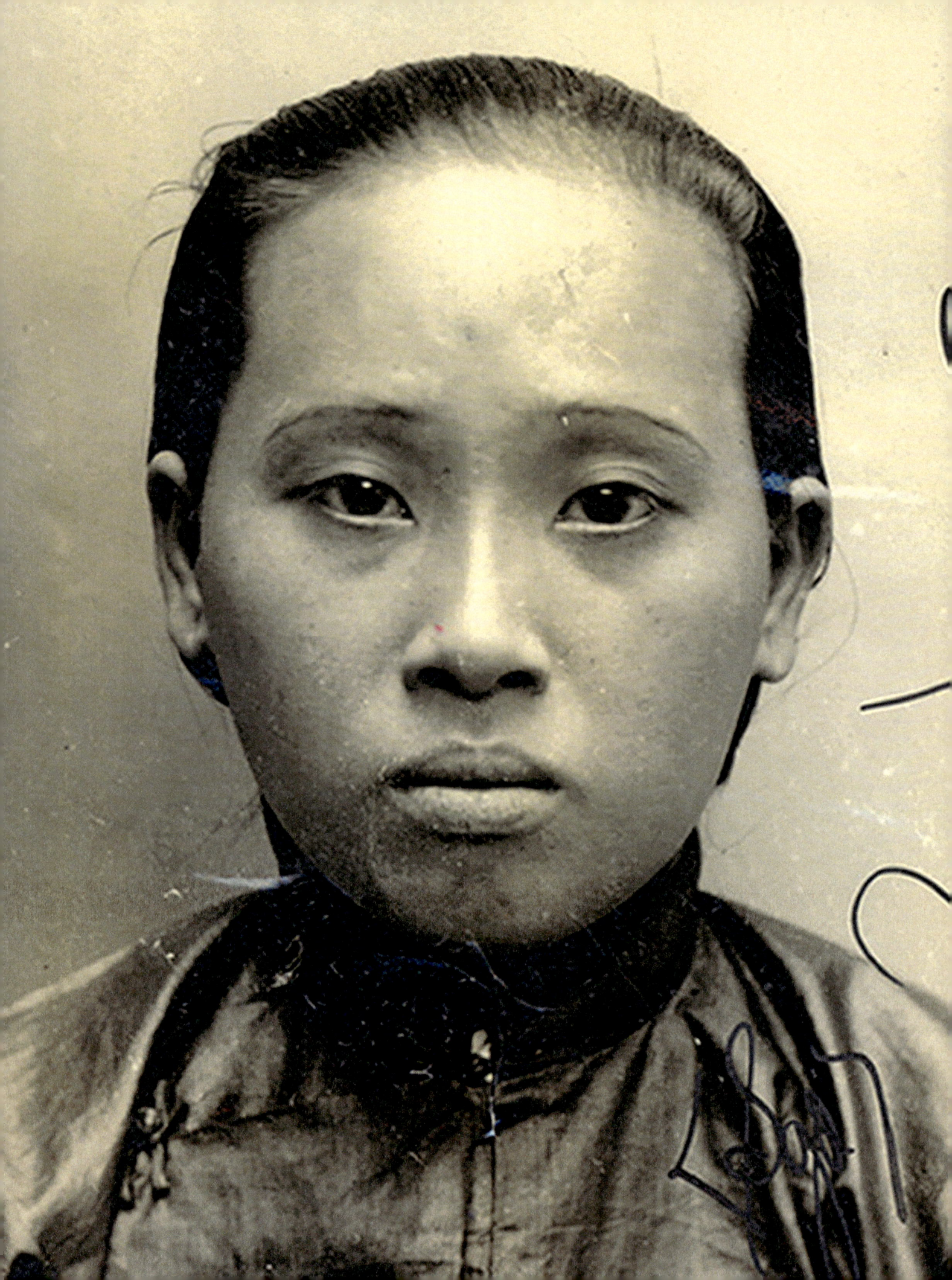

1916

Quok Shee was the longest involuntary resident of Angel Island.

Immigrant Quok Shee was the "alleged wife" of Chew Hoy Quong. When she arrived in San Francisco, she was detained and interrogated for nearly 2 years on Angel Island, mostly because Chinese women were suspected to be prostitutes in that era.

More than an inch thick, her "investigation case file" was opened in September 1916 and was not closed until August 1918. She was repeatedly interrogated, denied access to a lawyer, plagued by depression, subjected to smallpox, and was isolated from a husband who was her only contact in America, yet whom she hardly knew. The file contained 150 pages of legal maneuvering, inquisitorial interrogations, medical evaluations, intrigue court orders--all because one Chinese woman tried to enter the United States.In 1927, her husband Chew told immigration authorities that his wife had complained he was not giving her enough money and had run off with another man.

清朝腐敗，民不聊生，老百姓就算冒著生命危險， 也想盡辦法移民美國。天使島是中國移民要進入美國加州的第一道關卡，成千上萬的華人女性在此被拘禁，受盡屈辱。

20歲的郭氏（Quok Shee）於1916年到達舊金山，立刻被帶到天使島詢問。她的先生因為是美國合法居民，很快就被釋放了。但由於郭氏的答案與先生不符，因此被關了將近兩年。最後因為她的律師抗告移民局違反程序正義成功，郭氏終於重獲自由。沒人知道郭氏後來去了哪裡，只知道她丈夫在1927年向移民局報案，說他遭太太遺棄，因為郭氏抱怨他不給錢，所以跟別的男人跑了。

---

24. http://www.berkeley.edu/news/berkeleyan/2008/04/30_barde.shtml
25. http://archives.gov/publications/prologue/2004/spring/alleged-wife-1.html

1922

The Cable Act of 1922 forbade Chinese men from marrying white women.

The Anti-Miscegenation Act of 1889 prohibited Chinese men from marrying white women. The Cable Act of 1922 terminated citizenship of white American women who married Asian men. These laws were not fully overturned until the 1950s.

1889年的"反異種通婚法"禁止華人娶白人女性。1922年的克博法案（Cable Act of 1922）的成立，讓白人女性若嫁漢家郎就會喪失公民權。參議院於2014年5月16日正式為此法案道歉。

---

26. http://en.wikipedia.org/wiki/Cable_act

Martha Lum and sister

Martha Lum and sister attended public school for whites.

1927

Martha Lum was denied entry to a public school for white children.

In 1924, a nine-year old Chinese-American named Martha Lum was prohibited from attending Rosedale Consolidated High School in Bolivar County, Mississippi solely because she was of Chinese descent. The Supreme Court held that Gong Lum had not shown that there were not segregated schools accessible for the education of Martha Lum in Mississippi; therefore, Martha Lum was not allowed to go to the school for white children.

The picture directly below shows the two Lum sisters in third or fourth grade in the first row among white students. It was likely that the Supreme Court decision was not known in other local schools, for Gong Lum moved the family to Elaine, Arkansas where his girls attended white public schools. Lum v. Rice, 275 U.S. 78 (1927) was effectively overruled by the Court's decision in Brown v. Board of Education (1954), which outlawed segregation in public schools.

1924年，9歲的華人女孩 Martha Lum 想進密西西比州的洛斯戴爾學校（Rosedale School）就讀，但她的申請被拒。Martha Lum的母親是位受過高等教育的香港女性，她決定提起訴訟，強迫學校讓女兒上學，但最後沒能成功。最高法院判決Martha Lum不可就讀白人學校，但可以去上黑人及褐色人種的學校。

Martha Lum的父親發現各地對最高法院禁令的執行並不一致，所以把舉家遷到密西西比河對岸的阿肯色州的Elaine City，讓Martha Lum及她的姐姐得以就讀白人學校。1954年Brown v. Board of Education 一案終於判定公立學校的種族隔離政策為非法。

---

27. https://en.wikipedia.org/wiki/Lum_v._Rice
28. https://supreme.justia.com/cases/federal/us/275/78/case.html

TREATY BETWEEN THE REPUBLIC OF CHINA AND THE UNITED STATES
OF AMERICA FOR THE RELINQUISHMENT OF EXTRATERRITORIAL RIGHTS
IN CHINA AND THE REGULATION OF RELATED MATTERS

The Republic of China and the United States of America, desirous of emphasizing the friendly relations which have long prevailed between their two peoples and of manifesting their common desire as equal and sovereign States that the high principles in the regulation of human affairs to which they are committed shall be made broadly effective, have resolved to conclude a treaty for the purpose of adjusting certain matters in the relations of the two countries, and have appointed as their Plenipotentiaries:

The President of the National Government of the Republic of China,

    Dr. Wei Tao-ming, Ambassador Extraordinary and Plenipotentiary of the Republic of China to the United States of America, and

The President of the United States of America,

    Mr. Cordell Hull, Secretary of State of the United States of America;

Who, having communicated to each other their full powers found to be in due form, have agreed upon the following articles:

ARTICLE I. All those provisions of treaties or agreements in force between the Republic of China and the United States of America which authorize the Government of the United States of America or its representatives to exercise jurisdiction over nationals of the United States of America in the territory of the Republic of China are hereby abrogated. Nationals of the United States of America in such territory shall be subject to the jurisdiction of the Government of the Republic of China in accordance with the principles of international law and practice.

ARTICLE II. The Government of the United States of America considers that the Final Protocol concluded at Peking on September 7, 1901, between the Chinese Government and other governments, including the Government of the United States of America, should be terminated and agrees that the rights accorded to the Government of the United States of America under that Protocol and under agreements supplementary thereto shall cease.

The Government of the United States of America will cooperate with the Government of the Republic of China for the reaching of any necessary agreements with other governments concerned for the transfer to the Government of the Republic of China of the administration and control of the Diplomatic Quarter at Peiping, including the official assets and the official obligations of the Diplomatic Quarter, it being mutually understood that the Government of the Republic of China in taking over administration and control of the Diplomatic Quarter will make provision for the assumption and discharge of the official obligations and liabilities of the Diplomatic Quarter and for the recognition and protection of all legitimate rights therein.

The Government of the Republic of China hereby accords to the Government of the United States of America a continued right to use for official purposes the land which has been allocated to the Government of the United States of America in the diplomatic Quarter in Peiping, on parts of which are located buildings belonging to the Government of the United States

    nment of the United States of America considers
    lements at Shanghai and Amoy should revert to
    rol of the Government of the Republic of China
    accorded to the Government of the United States
    those Settlements shall cease.

1943

The 1943 Treaty was for the relinquishment of extraterritorial rights in China.

The Act repealed all the unfair treaties between China and the U.S. and allowed Chinese to immigrate for the first time since the Chinese Exclusion Act of 1882.

1939年第二次世界大戰爆發，中、英、美結為同盟國，美國因此廢除所有與中國之間的不平等條約。1943年蔣宋美齡被邀至美國國會演講，參議院藉她來訪之勢，一舉廢除排華法案。

Madam Chiang Kai-shek lectured in the Congress in 1943.

---

29. https://en.wikipedia.org/wiki/Sino-British_New_Equal_Treaty
30. http://www.chinaforeignrelations.net/node/215

1943

The Magnuson Act of 1950 encouraged Chinese to serve in the U.S. military in exchange for citizenship.

The Magnuson Act encouraged non-citizens, especially aliens whose skills were in languages and in medicine to serve in the U.S. military. A series of acts and agreements, such as The Lodge Act of 1950 and The Military Bases Agreement of 1947 were passed allowing non-citizens to serve in the U.S. military. During World War II, foreigners who served just three years in the military were entitled to citizenship. In 2013, Pentagon resumed a unique recruitment pilot program: the Military Accessions Vital to National Interest (MAVNI) aimed to recruit legal aliens whose skills (languages and medicine) were considered vital to national interest. Those recruited would be given an expedited path to U.S. citizenship.

麥諾森法案（Magnuson Act）及其他法案，如 Military Bases Agreement of 1947、Lodge Act of 1950，美國招募非公民參軍，答應迅速給予公民權。第二次世界大戰時，外國人從軍3年，即可獲得美國公民。2013年，美國防部再次招聘非公民參軍（MAVNI）計畫，特別是有外語及醫療能力的，他們可以在培訓10周後就成為公民（一般人要5年）。至2014年，在美國軍中服役的非公民軍人有24,000人，每年增加約5,000人。從2002至2013年，共有10,719名來至世界28國的人因加入美軍，成為美國公民。

---

31. https://en.wikipedia.org/wiki/Magnuson_Act

1943

Chinese American women were proudly served in the U.S. military.

In 1943, the Women's Army Corps recruited a unit of Chinese-American women to serve with the Army Air Forces as "Air WACs." The Army lowered the height and weight requirements for the women of this particular unit, referred to as the Madame Chiang Kai-Shek Air WAC unit. Air WACs served in a large variety of jobs, including aerial photo interpretation, air traffic control, and weather forecasting. WAC was dissolved in 1978.

1943年，一團華人女性加入美國空軍成為「Air WACs」，為了她們，空軍降低這團對高度及重量的要求，她們被稱為「蔣宋美齡空軍 WACs」，他們的工作包括對空圖的解釋、空中交通的控制及預報天氣。WAC 於1978年解散。

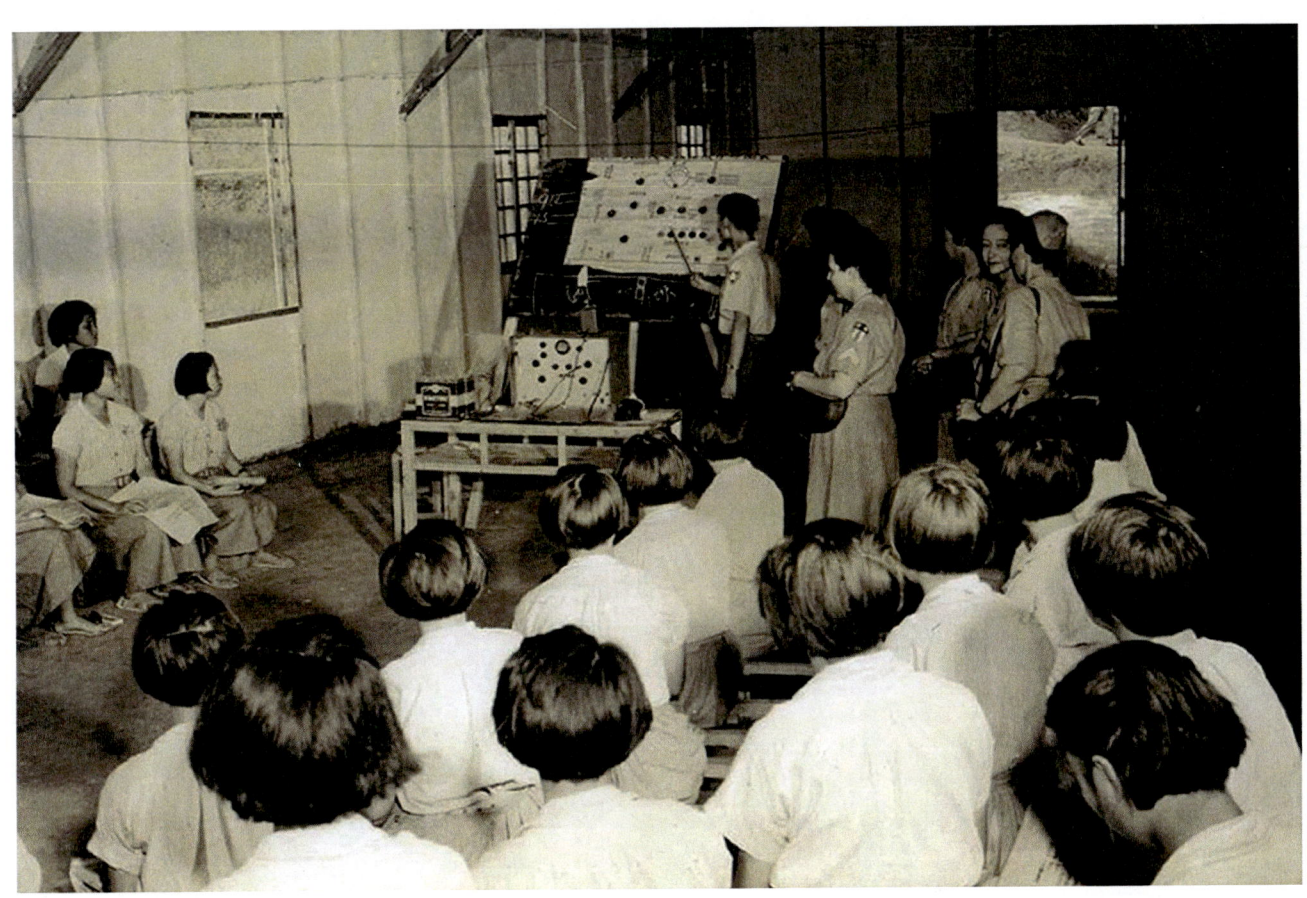

The Nisei WACs, Americans "with Japanese faces," were expected to show the Japanese what Americans of Japanese ancestry were like, and to help build bridges across a cultural gap. General MacArthur, however, did not approve of enlisted WACs serving overseas. He gave the women a choice of returning to the United States as WACs or being discharged from the Army and serving one-year contracts in Japan as civilians with US federal civil service status. All 13 agreed to stay in Japan as civil servants.

Nisei軍團被稱為有日本臉的美國人，其中包括日本人及中國人的後代，她們是為了溝通美日之間的文化差異而成軍的，但麥克阿瑟不贊成讓她們到海外服務，他給了這團女兵兩個選擇，一是回到美國繼續為WACs服務，或是從軍中退役，在日本服務一年。結果所有人都選擇留在日本。

Corporal Helen M. Lee of Willows, California, joined the WAC in August 1943 and was assigned to be the Chinese translator of GI training films at Lowry Army Air Field in California.

下士Helen M. Lee在1943年8月加入WACs（The Women's Army Corps），被派作中文翻譯人員。

Sergeant Julia (Larm) Ashford joined the WAC in 1944 and served in the Pacific Theater of Operations. She remained in the Army until 1948 when she enlisted in the newly formed Air Force where she served until 1953.

中士Julia Larm Ashford在1944年被派到德國占領區駐守，後於1953年退休。

A unique group of civilian women, Women Air Force Service Pilots (WASP) worked directly with the Army Air Forces on the home front during World War II flying planes from factories to air bases, testing planes for mechanical problems, and towing targets for aerial gunnery students to practice shooting. WASPs performed these dangerous assignments willingly.

During the years when male pilots were needed at the front. Thirty-eight WASP died in the line of duty, one being a Chinese-American, Hazel (Ying) Lee.

Lee flew pursuit (fighter) aircrafts from the production factories to air bases across the continental United States. She "named" the planes she flew by inscribing Chinese characters in lipstick on the tails. Her husband was an officer in the Chinese Air Force. Lee died in a two-plane crash when her plane and that of a colleague received identical instructions from an air traffic controller on their approach to Great Falls AFB, Montana.

美國民間組織成了一個女子航空勤務飛行隊（Women Air Force Service Pilots，WASP）。這些女性為空軍飛行員服務，她們將飛機從工廠飛到空軍基地測試機械問題，為射擊訓練空投目標。當時因為男性都必須上前線，WASP就自願做這些危險任務，38位WASP成員在執行任務時死亡，其中一位就是 Hazel Ying Lee。

Hazel Ying Lee 開了一架戰鬥機，從製造廠開到空軍基地來，橫跨美國的州際，並以中文命名這架戰鬥機，還把機名用口紅寫在機尾。後來她開的飛機跟同事開的飛機對撞，在蒙塔那州 Great Falls 壯烈犧牲。

Maggie Gee started as a mechanical draftsman at Mare Island, California. She was accepted by the WASP. She took military pilots up for qualifying flights to renew their instrument ratings and co-piloted B-17 Flying Fortress bombers through mock dogfights staged to train bomber gunners.

朱美嬌（Maggie Gee）1923年生於加州柏克萊市，年少時就有志於開飛機的夢想，於1944年3月加入女子航空勤務飛行隊（WASP），被分派到內華達州內利斯空軍基地，接受飛行員軍事訓練。

Army nurse Helen (Pon) Onyett risked her life tending wounded soldiers from the landing craft that came ashore in North Africa. She was awarded the Legion of Merit for her actions during the war and retired from the Corps as a full colonel.

Helen Pon Onyett 是位護士，她在北非照顧從飛機降落時受傷的軍人，出色的表現讓她在退休時被晉升為上校。

Gail (Chin) Wong, a Chinese-American, served from 1945-1949. She later worked in a Veterans Administration hospital from 1972 until her retirement in 1988.

Gail Chin Wong 在退伍軍人醫院工作，直到 1988 年退休。

Although the Navy refused to accept Japanese-American women throughout World War II, some Chinese-American women volunteered to serve. Marietta (Chong) Eng decided to enlist in the WAVES. The Navy trained Eng as an occupational therapist. Eng helped rehabilitate sailors and officers who had lost arms and legs in the war, teaching them to accomplish the many tasks of daily living.

Marietta Chong Eng 是位軍中的物理治療師。她出生於夏威夷，決定從軍是因為她弟弟已在海軍。她協助斷手斷腳的海軍及軍官重新學習如何處理日常生活中的活動。

Rita Chow joined the US Army Nurse Corps in 1954 as a second lieutenant. The Army assigned her as a Medical Surgery Nursing Instructor at Fitzsimmons Army Hospital in Denver, Colorado. She was soon promoted to first lieutenant and became an instructor to medical corpsmen at Brooke Army Medical Center, Fort Sam Houston, San Antonio, Texas. She was discharged from active duty in 1958 and spent the next 11 years in the Army Reserve.

Rita Chow在1954年是少尉，同年加入美國護士隊，並被陸軍指派為醫療外科護理學講師。1958年轉入後勤服務。

Colonel Yeu-Tsu "Margaret" Lee, US Army Medical Corps, graduated from Harvard Medical School and was a female surgeon.

She was one of four active duty surgeons assigned to the 13th Evacuation Hospital during Operation Desert Storm. Before World War II, American medical schools did not accept female students. Most of the males went to fight the war during World War II, which create a shortage of men. Medical schools had no alternative but to accept female medical students.

李雨珠（Yeu-Tsu）畢業於哈佛醫學院，是女外科醫師，也是海灣戰爭中美軍上校女博士。

在第二次世界大戰以前，美國醫學院是不招收女生的。二次大戰期間許多男生都去打仗了，醫學院才開始招收女生。李雨珠讀的班裡有90位學生，只有6位女生。最後李雨珠定居在夏威夷。

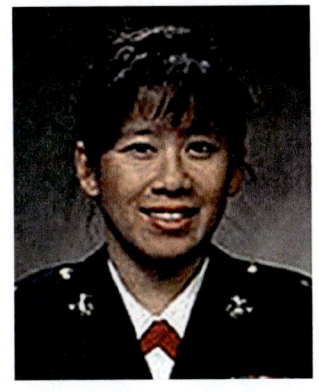

Captain Melissa Kuo of Manchester, Connecticut, joined the Marine Corps in 1992 and served on active duty until 1996.

上尉Melissa Kuo於1992年加入海軍，1996年退伍。

---

32. http://www.womensmemorial.org/Education/APA.html

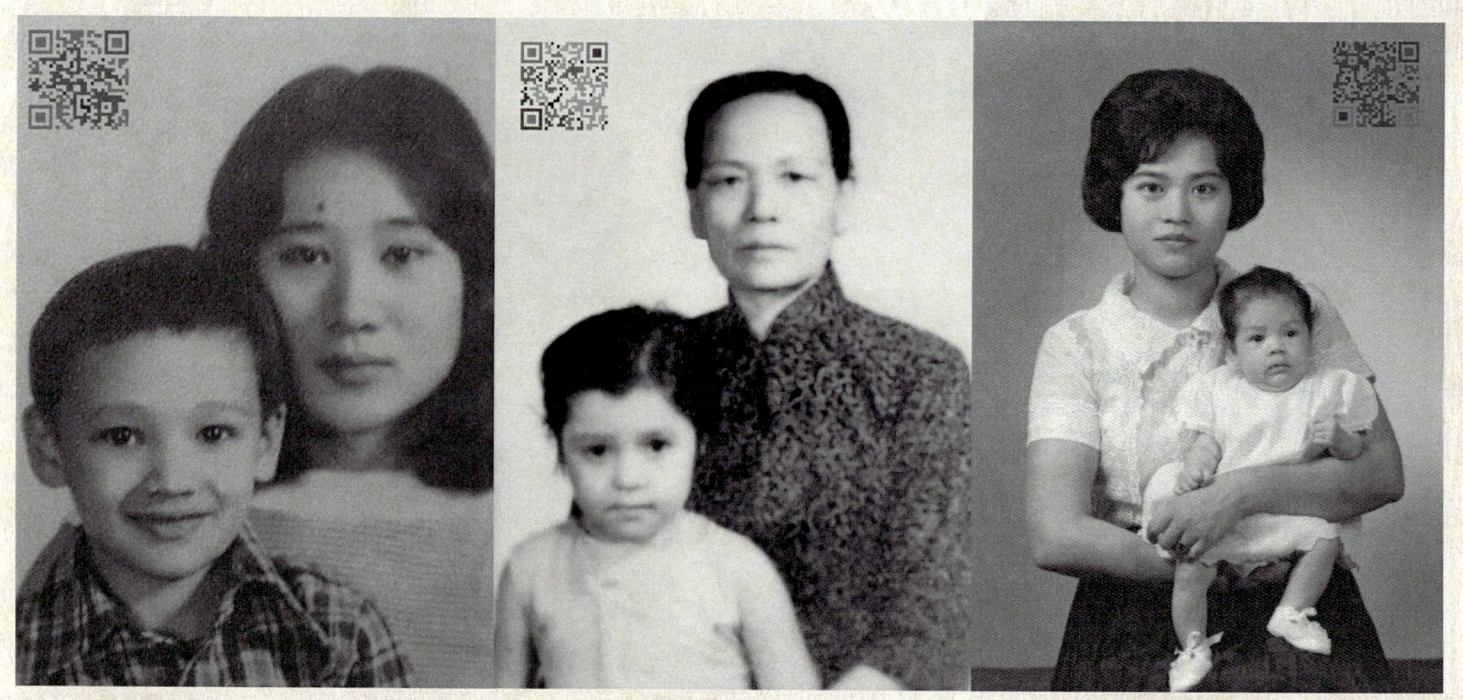

1945

Stories of three Amerasians

After World War II, American soldiers fathered many mixed-parentage children who were not accepted by the local Asian communities. Because of their torment, Congress passed the "War Brides Act" to bring them back to the land of their fathers. But no more than 3 percent found their fathers in their adoptive homeland. In 1982, Congress passed "Public Law 97-359" which officially defined "Ameriasians" as those born in Asia to a U.S. military father and an Asian mother. The law allowed them to become U.S. citizens. Examples of well-known Ameriasians are entertainers Lai Pei-Xia, Tien LuLu, Tony Wang and sportsman Zhi-long Zhen.

1939到1945年，美軍與亞洲當地的婦女所生的後代，因為不容於當地社會，美國國會遂通過「戰爭新娘法（War Brides Act of 1946）」，讓這群出生於亞洲的混血兒，得以踏上父親的國土，但只有3%的父親出面相認。越戰後，國會再於1982年通過「公法97-359（Public Law 97-359）」，正式定義「亞美混血兒」，讓他們得以移民美國。沒人知道亞美混血兒的正確數字，除了越南、菲律賓、日本，台灣也有亞美混血兒。當年曾有20萬人次的韓戰、越戰美軍來台休假，在20年間生出成千上萬的亞美混血兒。著名的亞美混血如歌手賴佩霞、田路路、王湯尼和曾任台灣立法委員的鄭志龍。

---

33. http://en.wikipedia.org/wiki/War_Brides_Act
34. http://www.chinainsight.info/culture/chinese/202-chinese-american-immigration-timeline.html
35. http://library.uwb.edu/guides/usimmigration/1946_alien_fiancees_and_fiances_act.html

My mother is a stranger.

They said my father was an American soldier stationed in Taiwan in 1958. My mother met him at a bar and I was born the next year. I have never met my father, I don't even know his name.

My mother went to Japan to make a better living soon after I was born, my grandma raised me. She passed away when I was 13, my mother came back for the funeral, she promised to adopt me and even hired a lawyer for my immigration. The lawyer later told me that my mother had terminated his service, and that I would not be going to America. As an adult, I became a singer and went to Washington D.C. to perform for a group of overseas Chinese. I got the news that my mother wanted to see me. We finally met, the media went berserk, but I did not feel anything. We met in the hotel for a few minutes and parted. I have never seen her since.

田路路（Tien Lu-Lu）聽說她的父親是駐台美國大兵，母親是1958年在酒吧裡遇見他的，次年田路路就誕生了。

田路路出生不久，母親就到國外去謀生，把她交給外婆撫養，祖孫兩人相依為命。外婆常常替她染髮，不希望她被認出是混血兒。田路路13歲那年，外婆去世了，母親回來奔喪，她本來答應收養田路路，後來卻變卦了。13歲的田路路及時參加演藝工作，養活自己。因為她出色的五官及外貌，事業一度相當成功。有一次她到美國去宣慰僑胞，忽然接到母親要和她見面的訊息，兩人在機場見面，互相擁抱，旁觀的人都感動流淚，但田路路和母親完全無感，母女倆就再也沒有見過面了。

Tien Lulu and her grandma

Lai Pei-Xia was her mother's baby doll.

Lai Pei-Sha 's mother worked as a helper for an American military family in Taipei. She noticed how respectful American men treated women. She was especially fond of their children with blue eyes and blond hair. She called them "baby doll", and she decided one day to have one her own. She later met Lai Pei-Sha's father who was a friend of her employer.

Once Lai Pei-Sha was born, she was the baby doll her mother always dreamed of. Eventually Lai Pei-Sha found her father in the U.S. Despite the reunion, Lai Pei-Sha never talked about her father afterwards.

賴佩霞（Lai Pei-Shia）的母親曾在美國軍官家裡幫忙，她發現美國男人對女性特別尊重，他們金髮藍眼的小孩也非常可愛，於是她決定有一天也要生一個洋娃娃。後來她碰到賴佩霞的生父，賴佩霞就誕生了。

從來沒見過父親的賴佩霞，因緣際會找到了與生父聯絡的方式，她和母親於是展開萬里尋父之旅。賴佩霞當時的想法很簡單，就只是想看看自己的父親。沒想到接電話的那頭是父親現任的太太。父女重逢場面十分尷尬，但當兩人單獨相處時，雙方都哭紅了眼，賴佩霞當初在腦海裡演練過千遍的重逢畫面，早已忘的一乾二淨。只是，賴佩霞從此再也沒有跟任何人談起她的父親。

Lei Pei-Xia and her mother

Tony Wang was reunited with his father after 41 years.

Tony was born in 1973 to an American soldier stationed in Tainan and a Taiwanese mother. Although Tony never met his father, as long as he could remember, his only dream was to find him.

Shortly after Tony's birth, his mother left him to seek a better life in Japan and he was placed with her friend Po Po in Taichung. Luckily for Tony, he grew up with plenty of love and attention from Po Po and her family. As an adult, Tony catapulted to stardom as an award-winning rock musician. Despite fame & fortune, he still longed to know the father he never knew. Fast forward to 2014, Tony met Dr. Chang C. Chen, an American lawyer who was doing research on the subject of Amerasians for this exhibit. Tony gave Dr. Chen the only information he had on his father —a piece of paper with "W. D. Brown, Texas" written on the corner.

Dr. Chen tracked down 46 people with exactly the same name in Texas. Someone from the Facebook page "Tainan AB" tipped off Dr. Chen that Tony's father could be the W.D. Brown in Cincinnati. Dr. Chen reached out to him. Her calls went unanswered. As a last ditch effort, she suggested to Tony, "Why don't you leave him a message, and if he does not answer, we know he does not want to acknowledge your existence." Her strategy worked. W. D. Brown returned Tony's call the very next day.

Father and son were tearfully reunited on August 1, 2014 via Skype. In November 15, 2014, W.D. Brown visited Tony in Taiwan, 41 years after he left.

Tony Wang and mother.

王湯尼（Tony Wang）生於1973年，父親是駐台南美軍。父親在他出生之前被調離台灣，母親隨後到日本去謀生。住在台中的母親友人「婆婆」盡心將他撫養成人。

王湯尼於2014年遇到美國律師邱彰，後者正在做亞美混血兒的研究。王湯尼給了邱彰他手上唯一有關於父親的一紙資訊：「W. D. Brown, Texas」。

邱彰後來在德州找到46位同名同姓的人，經過台南美軍臉書網頁 Tainan AB 管理人指認現在住在辛辛那提的王湯尼生父，父子兩人於2014年8月1日涕淚交流的在網路上相認，同年11月15日，王湯尼的父親千里迢迢的趕來台灣與41歲的湯尼見面。

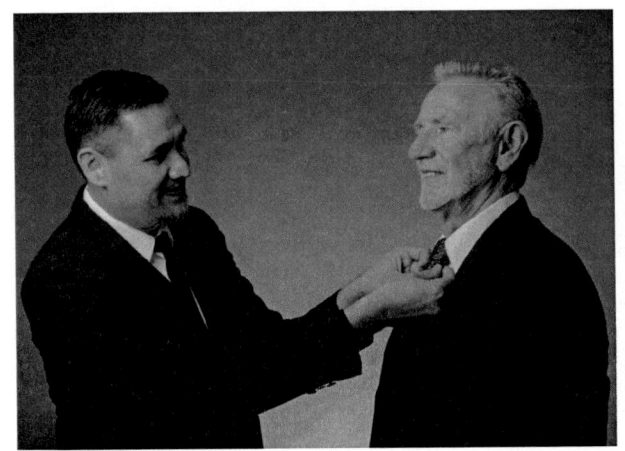 

Tony Wang reunited with his father.

1953

Eileen Chan became U.S. citizen under the Refugee Relief Act of 1953.

Under The Refugee Relief Act of 1953, a refugee is defined as someone who lacks the essentials of life. There was a 2,000 refugee quota allocated to the Chinese living in Hong Kong. Famous writer Eileen Chang applied in 1955 under this Act and her application was approved quickly. Many of Eileen Chang works were made into movies including Li Ang's "Lust, Caution".

1953年，美國國會通過「難民救濟法」，給難民簽證。根據該法，難民的定義是缺乏生存必須物的人，審查過程非常嚴格。該法實施至1956年，共准許了214,000位難民移民美國，其中2,000名是給居住在香港的中國內地人。大文學家張愛玲（Eileen Chang）於1952到1955年間住在香港。她在1955年根據「難民救濟法」提出申請移民美國，由於當時美國新聞處處長麥卡錫做她的擔保人，所以很快就被批准了。張愛玲一生著作甚豐，書迷遍及全世界，許多作品被拍成電影，如李安導演的「色，戒」。

 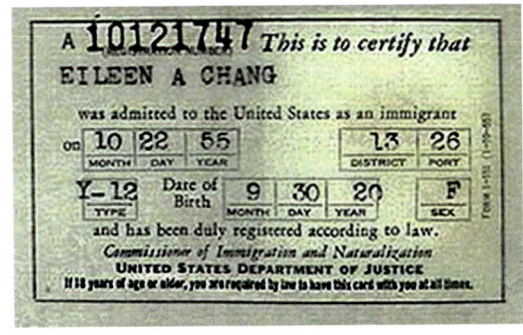

Eileen Chang's green card

---

36. https://en.wikipedia.org/wiki/Eileen_Chang

1964

Civil Rights Act was passed in 1964.

The Civil rights movement was at its peak when Dr. Martin Luther King delivered his famous "I have a dream" speech on August 28, 1963. Three months later, President John F. Kennedy was murdered and the Civil Rights Act of 1964 was passed. The Act outlaws discrimination based on race, color, religion, sex, or national origin. It ended unequal application of voter registration requirements and racial segregation in schools, at the workplace and public accommodations.

1964年，民權運動因金恩博士發表「我有一個夢」的演說而進入高潮。同年，甘迺迪總統被殺，民權法案終於通過，從此不得因種族、膚色、宗教、性別、國籍而歧視，也不得在投票時、或在學校及公共場所，因種族因素而實施任何差別待遇。

---

37. https://en.wikipedia.org/wiki/Civil_Rights_Act_of_1964

1965

The Immigration and Nationality Act of 1965 changed the face of the American population.

The Immigration and Nationality Act of 1965 marked fundamental changes in America's immigration policy. Immigration increased fourfold in five years. The Act abolished the national origins quota system started in the 1920's, and replaced it with a system that focused on immigrants' skills and family relationships with citizens or U.S. residents.

During the debate of this law on the Senate floor, Senator Ted Kennedy, speaking of the effects of the Act, said, "...our cities will not be flooded with a million immigrants annually.... Secondly, the ethnic mix of this country will not be upset...." These assertions would later prove grossly inaccurate. The 1965 Act had greatly changed the face of the American population. Minority had become majority in many states and partially resulting in the election of the first black American President Barrack Obama.

1965年「美國移民與國籍法」是影響美國移民政策最重要的移民法，過去的大熔爐理論被「沙拉拼盤」的新概念所取代，使得各民族仍能保有它的文化特色。該法改變了1920年以來以「國籍」為主的移民政策，歡迎有「專業能力」的人移民。

當年極力推動本法的參議員泰德‧甘迺迪曾向國會保證：美國人口的組成不會受到影響，也不會影響白人的生計。法案執行的結果正好相反。此法通過後，移民人數在五年內增加四倍，以亞州及中南美州移民最多，少數民族在許多州成為多數，並促成歐巴馬於 2008 年被選為第一位黑人美國總統。

---

38. INS, Act of 1965, Pub.L. 89-236
39. President Lyndon B Johnson's Remarks at the Signing of the Immigration Bill, Liberty Island, New York". October 3, 1965. http://www.lbjlib.utexas.edu/Johnson/archives.hom/speeches.hom/651003.asp
40. Jennifer Ludden. "1965 immigration law changed face of America"
41. http://ndn.org/taxonomy/term/940
42. Gabriel J. Chin, "The Civil Rights Revolution Comes to Immigration Law: A New Look at the Immigration and Nationality Act of 1965"North Carolina Law Review, Vol. 75, p. 273, 1996
43. http://papers.ssrn.com/sol3/papers.cfm?abstract_id=1121504

1967

Freedom to marry was upheld in Loving v. Virginia, 388 U.S. 1 (1967)

Loving v. Virginia is a landmark civil rights decision of the United States Supreme Court which invalidated laws prohibiting interracial marriage. The case was brought by Mildred Loving, a black woman, and Richard Loving, a white man, who had been sentenced to a year in prison in Virginia for marrying each other. Their marriage violated the state's anti-miscegenation statute, the Racial Integrity Act of 1924, which prohibited marriage between people classified as "white" and people classified as "colored". The Supreme Court's unanimous decision determined that this prohibition was unconstitutional, reversing Pace v. Alabama (1883) and ending all race-based legal restrictions on marriage in the United States.

在美國各州，異族通婚一直被視為非法，直到1958年，黑白通婚的愛夫婦提起訴訟，最高法院認定婚姻乃基本人權，所以各州禁止異族通婚的法律一律違憲。愛夫婦不是華人，卻為華人爭取到最基本的婚姻權。

---

44. Loving v. Virginia, 388 U.S. 1 (1967)
45. https://en.wikipedia.org/wiki/Loving_v._Virginia

1974

Lau v. Nichols, 414 U.S. 563 (1974) helped shape the bilingual education system.

In 1974, the Supreme Court ruled in Lau v. Nichols, 414 U.S. 563 (1974) that school districts must help non-English speaking students learn English. This case reflects the changes in cultural perspectives towards diversity and immigration. The Bilingual Education Act was passed and the school districts were directly funded by the federal government.

劉訴尼考爾斯案是由舊金山華人學生提告的,因為他們英文不流利,在受教育的權利上被歧視。最高法院判決,英語非母語的學生可受到特別輔導及雙語教育,聯邦並通過「Bilingual Education Act」,由聯邦政府直接補助各地學區,使得英語非母語的學生都有機會及資源學習英文。

---

46. https://supreme.justia.com/cases/federal/us/414/563/case.html
47. https://en.wikipedia.org/wiki/Lau_v._Nichols

1977

Mi Chu won her employment with the Library of Congress under the Equal Employment Opportunity Act of 1972.

Mi Chu was the first Chinese-American woman to win a sex discrimination lawsuit under the Equal Employment Opportunity Act.

Originally from Taiwan, she obtained a Ph.D. from Harvard University. In 1977, she applied for a job as a librarian with the Library of Congress. She was denied even an interview. She sued and won a sex discrimination-in-employment case against the Library of Congress (Mi Chu Wiens, Plaintiff v. Daniel J. Boorstin, Defendant, Civil Action No. 78–1034, U.S. District Court for the District of Columbia). Her lawyer sent her a note: "Think of it, Mi Chu Wiens has defeated the United States of America."

She worked in the Library of Congress for 35 years and retired in 2012.

居蜜（Chu Mi）畢業於台大，擁有哈佛大學的碩士及博士學位，精通中英法三國語言，任職副教授，也有許多專業著作。

1977年，她向美國國會圖書館亞洲部求職，連面試的機會都被拒絕，館方的理由是她缺乏3年專業職等的經驗。居蜜於是向聯邦法院提起性別歧視訴訟，法官發現被雇用的男士的專業程度與經驗比不上居蜜，違反1964年「民權法」以及1972年「就業機會平等法」，因此將此職位判給了居蜜。她的律師寫字條給她：想想看，居蜜竟然打贏了美國政府。

居蜜後來在國會圖書館工作35年，於2012年退休。

---

48. Civil Action No. 78-1034, U.S. District Court for the District of Columbia,1979 U.S. Dist. LEXIS 14815；19 Fair Empl. Prac. Cas.(BNA) 186； 19 Empl. Prac. Dec. (CCH) P9003
49. http://www.chinatimes.com/newspapers/20141201000369-260106

1979

Patricia Cowett was the first Chinese-American judge.

Patricia Yim Cowett became the first Chinese-American woman judge when she was appointed by California Governor Brown as San Diego Superior Court judge.

第一位華裔女性法官嚴美玉（Patricia Cowett）在1979年就職，由當時加州州長布朗任命為聖地牙哥市立法院法官。

---

50. http://www.calbar.ca.gov/AboutUs/JudicialNomineesEvaluation/Roster/PatriciaCowett.aspx

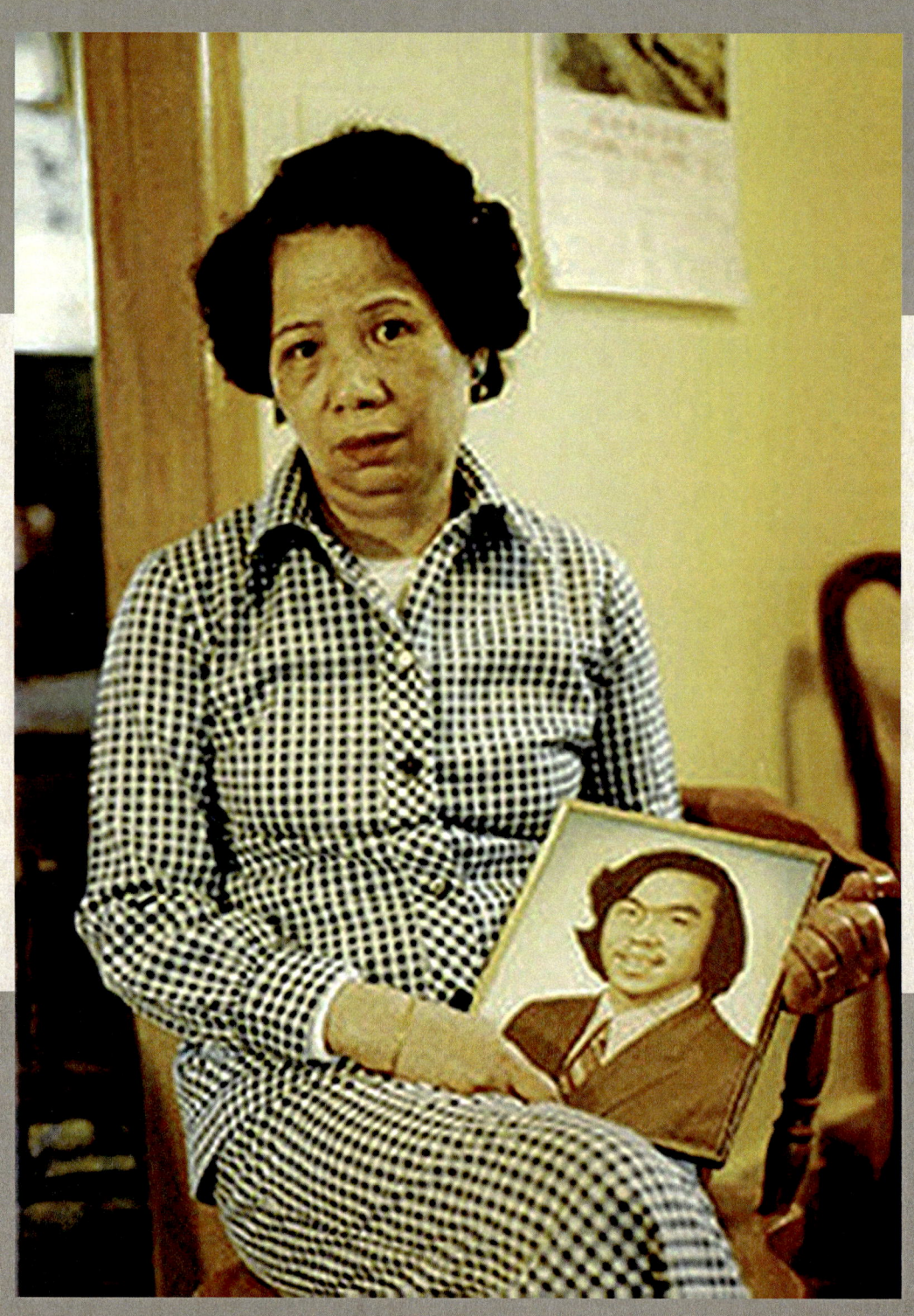

1982

Vincent Chin's murder was a hate-crime.

Due to the increasing sales of Japanese cars to the U.S., in 1979, many autoworkers in Detroit were laid off. Vincent Chin, then 27 years old, received racially charged comments and was beaten to death. Two perpetrators Ebens and Nitz received lenient sentencing in a plea bargain which caused public outrage. The case became a rallying point for the Asian American community. Ebens and Nitz were put on trial for violating Chin's civil rights.

Because the subsequent federal prosecution was the result of public pressure from a coalition of many Asian ethnic organizations, Vincent Chin's murder is often considered the beginning of a pan-ethnic Asian American movement. Christine Choy and Renee Tajima-Pena produced a documentary "Who Killed Vincent Chin?" and it was nominated for an Academy Award for Best Documentary Feature in 1987.

1979年日本車大量銷美，美國汽車工人失業並失控。1982年，27歲的陳果仁被失業的白人汽車工人打死，兇嫌被判無罪，華人社區震怒。後來經過華人社團極力爭取，本案由聯邦檢察官提起公訴，並被定位為種族仇恨犯罪。

陳母余瓊芳（Lily Chin），在陳果仁6歲時從一家香港的孤兒院領養他。案發後，她向兇嫌提起民事求償，裁定得賠145萬美元，但兇嫌無力支付，至今已累積超過500萬美元。余瓊芳不堪觸景傷情，離美返回中國，她於2002年去世，在去世前她設立陳果仁獎學金。Christine Choy 和 Renee Tajima-Pena製作的紀錄片「誰殺了陳果仁？（Who Killed Vincent Chin？）」獲得1987年奧斯卡最佳紀錄片獎提名。

---

51. Henry Yee and the Estate of Vincent Chin (deceased) vs. Roald Ebens, Michael Nitz, and Fancy Pants Lounge, 83-309788 CZ(Mich 3 rd Cir.1983)
52. https://en.wikipedia.org/wiki/Murder_of_Vincent_Chin

1983

Lily Lee Chen became the first Chinese American woman mayor.

Lily Lee Chen was born in Tianjin and raised in Taiwan. In 1958, she came to the U.S. for her graduate study of social work. In 1966 when she started to work for the Los Angeles County, social work had already become a red-hot career track for aspiring politicians. She used the grassroots approach and won the respect of her community. In 1983, Lily Lee Chen was elected mayor of Monterey Park, California and became the first Chinese American mayor.

陳李琬若（Lily Lee Chen）出生於天津，1948年隨父母遷至台灣。1958年留學美國，學習冷門的社工系，得到碩士學位。1966年起，她任職於洛杉磯郡政府，當時社工人員已成為最熱門的行業。做為社工人員，她於基層做起，一步一腳印，贏得當地居民的信任，在1983年被選為加州蒙特利公園市（Monterey Park）市長，並成為美國史上首位華裔女市長。在美國政壇上，蒙特利公園市市長的職位不高，但陳李琬若利用她的高媒體曝光率，為華裔爭取了許多福利，例如她協助把「亞裔」正式列為美國法律上的少數族裔，使亞裔美人得以享受各種福利。

---

53. https://committee100.org/aboutus/member_bio.php?member_id=22

1993

Sister Ping smuggled all the villagers from Shengmei, Fujian Province to America.

In 1993, over two hundred Chinese were smuggled on board of a cargo ship named Golden Venture. The ship run aground off the beaches of Queens, leaving passengers struggling in the freezing water. Ten people drowned. The smuggling was arranged by a stocky 56 years old Sister Ping from Manhattan's Chinatown. She was uneducated, did not speak English, but according to the U.S. Department of Justice, her international human smuggling operation is one of the first, and ultimately most successful, alien smugglers of all time. She made over $40 million USD for these operations from 1984 to 2000. She bought the Golden Venture solely for the use of alien smuggling.

Her customers said the reason they fled China was because of the One Child policy, they were not allowed to have more than one child. Hoping to have more children, all the villagers of Shengmei left. The FBI had been following Sister Ping since 1990. In 2000, she was arrested in Hong Kong, and eventually extradited to New York. She was convicted in June 2005 and was sentenced to 35 years in prison. She died in the U.S. Federal prison in April 2014. Thousands attended her funeral, villagers from Shengmei called her a living Buddha. The Golden Venture was deliberately sunk on August 22, 2000.

1993年，「金色冒險號」的偷渡客在紐約外海冰冷的海水中掙扎，此時曼哈頓的中國城有一位矮胖的女士－56歲的鄭翠屏，人稱「萍姐（Sister Ping）」，正在家裡看電視。她沒有受過教育，不會說英文，但靠替人偷渡，賺了四千萬美金，「金色冒險號」是她出資購買的。美國檢調單位稱她為「蛇頭之母」，她的偷渡網遍及全世界。

偷渡客說他們之所以逃離中國，是因為一胎化政策強迫墮胎，雖然他們知道到美國後會受苦，但因為可以生孩子，人生總算有了希望。大家的想法都一樣，中國福建有幾個村子，整個村子人都走光了。「金色冒險號」會出事，是因為蛇頭間發生間隙，互相謀殺。但萍姐不知道FBI從1990年就開始跟監她了。2005年，陪審團認定萍姐偷渡、綁架、洗錢等罪名成立，判刑35年，後來死在獄中。萍姐的喪禮，萬人空巷，福建家鄉人還自願代她服刑，說她是活菩薩。「金色冒險號」後來被美國政府擊沉。

---

54. https://en.wikipedia.org/wiki/Sister_Ping

2000

Florence Fang became owner of a mainstream newspaper—the San Francisco Examiner.

Florence Fang owns The Independent newspaper, a chain of eight Peninsula weeklies. On March 17, 2000, she successfully bought a mainstream newspaper, the San Francisco Examiner, and became the first Chinese-American chairwoman of the board.

Former President George H.W. Bush said: "America is a tale of immigrants who came to this land to build a nation and better their own lives. The Florence Fang story is yet another chapter on the American experience. Her pursuit and fulfillment of the American dream serves as a reminder that America is truly the land of opportunity."

2000年3月17日,來自台灣的方李邦琴(Florence Fang)主掌的「獨立報(Indepent)」,成功的收購了美國主流英文報「舊金山觀察家報(San Francisco Examiner)」,並成為這家英文報紙的第一位女性華人董事長。

美國前總統喬治布希說:「美國是移民在一片土地上建設家園、美好自己生活的一個童話,方李邦琴的故事就是這童話中的一章。方李邦琴的美國圓夢證明了美國仍然是一個充滿機會的地方。」

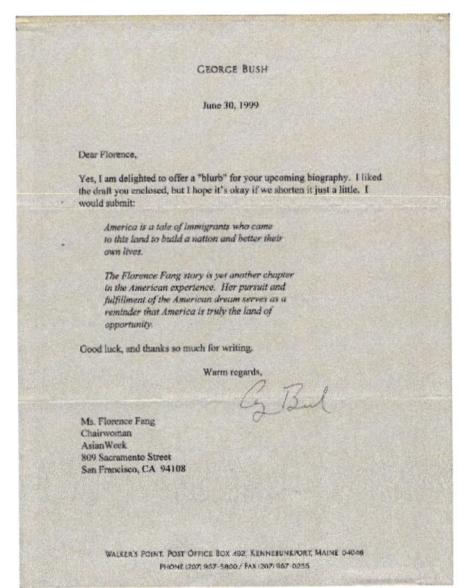

55. http://florencefangfamilyfoundation.org/index.php/2014-08-15-02-16-03

2001

Elaine Chao was the first Chinese-American woman cabinet secretary.

Elaine Chao served as the 24th United States Secretary of Labor in the cabinet of President George W. Bush from 2001 to 2009. She was the first Chinese-American woman to be appointed to a President's cabinet.

趙小蘭（Elaine L. Chao）出生於台北，8歲時移居美國。1987年獲選美國十大傑出女性青年。趙小蘭最早接觸政治是在1983年雷根總統主政期間，當時她被選為白宮學者，負責政策分析與研究。後於1986年進入美國聯邦政府，擔任聯邦運輸部副部長，當時已是聯邦政府中職位最高的華人女性。趙小蘭於2001年被布希總統提名，並於1月29日獲得聯邦參議員全票通過，成為美國第24任勞工部長。

---

56. https://en.wikipedia.org/wiki/Elaine_Chao

2009

2009

Dolly Gee became the first female Chinese-American federal judge.

Judy Chu was the first Chinese-American Congresswoman.

Dolly Gee is the Federal District Court judge for the Central District Court of California. She was nominated by President Obama and approved by the entire Senate in 2009.

Judy May Chu was the first Chinese-American woman ever elected to the U.S. Congress. On June 18, 2012, the United States House of Representatives passed a resolution introduced by Congresswoman Chu that formally expressed the regret of the House of Representatives for the Chinese Exclusion Act.

2009年，朱美瑜（Dolly Gee）經由歐巴馬總統提名，參議院全票通過，成為美國第一位華裔女性聯邦法院法官，任職於加州中區聯邦法院。

趙美心（Judy Chu），1953年生於美國加州，她代表民主黨在加利福尼亞州第32選區當選聯邦眾議員，成為歷史上第一位華裔女性眾議員。美國眾議院於2012年6月18日通過趙美心的提案，正式向全體華人為當年的排華法案表示遺憾。

57. https://en.wikipedia.org/wiki/Judy_Chu
https://en.wikipedia.org/wiki/Judy_Chu

58. https://en.wikipedia.org/wiki/Dolly_M._Gee

CALIFORNIA LEGISLATURE

Assembly

RESOLUTION

By the Honorable Paul Fong, 22nd Assembly District; and the Honorable Kevin de León, 45th Assembly District; and the following Assembly Coauthors: Assembly Members Furutani, Lieu, Torrico, Adams, Ammiano, Arambula, Bass, Beall, Bill Berryhill, Tom Berryhill, Blakeslee, Block, Blumenfield, Brownley, Buchanan, Caballero, Charles Calderon, Carter, Chesbro, Conway, Cook, Coto, Davis, De La Torre, DeVore, Duvall, Emmerson, Eng, Evans, Feuer, Fletcher, Fuentes, Gaines, Gilmore, Hagman, Hall, Harkey, Hayashi, Hernandez, Hill, Huber, Huffman, Jeffries, Jones, Krekorian, Logue, Bonnie Lowenthal, Ma, Mendoza, Miller, Monning, Nava, Nestande, Niello, Nielsen, John A. Perez, V. Manuel Perez, Ruskin, Salas, Saldana, Silva, Skinner, Smyth, Solorio, Audra Strickland, Swanson, Torlakson, Torres, Tran, Villines, and Yamada; and the following Senate Coauthors: Senators Liu and Yee; Relative to

Chinese Americans in California

Whereas, The California gold rush triggered one of the largest mass migrations in world history and captured global imagination as the destination for wealth and opportunity. That global migration made California one of the world's most diverse states which would serve as the foundation for its economic, academic, and cultural growth in the 20th century; and

Whereas, The California gold rush paved the way in funding and manpower for the creation and building of the western leg of the transcontinental railroad. The transcontinental railroad was considered the greatest American technological feat of the 19th century, was a dream of Abraham Lincoln's, and was what many considered the most important aspect in strengthening the position of the United States in the international spotlight. The track served as a vital link for trade, commerce, and travel by joining east and west, further transforming the population and economy of California; and

Whereas, The Central Pacific portion of the transcontinental railroad recruited the Chinese in America and later tens of thousands of Chinese immigrants as a source of labor. Chinese in America and Chinese immigrants were paid less than their white counterparts and slept in tents while white laborers were provided both food and shelter. The Chinese laborers worked under grueling and treacherous conditions in order to lay thousands of miles of track. On May 10, 1868, alone, Chinese workers laid 10 miles of track in less than 12 hours in order to complete the last leg of the railroad. Without the tremendous efforts and contributions of the Chinese in building the transcontinental railroad, the development and progress of our nation and California would have been delayed by years; and

Whereas, Once the transcontinental railroad was complete, Chinese in California transitioned to other types of employment, making considerable contributions to the progress and growth of our state. Chinese in California built ships for fishing along our coast and developed the abalone and shrimp industries. In the Delta and the central valley, the Chinese in California helped to recover the tule swamps, to build irrigation systems, and to harvest various fruits and vegetables for California's agriculture industry; and

Whereas, The Legislature enacted discriminatory laws targeting Chinese in America and Chinese immigrants in order to discourage further immigration from China, and sought to severely limit the success of the Chinese laborers already here; and

Whereas, Among other things, these laws denied the Chinese in California the right to own land or property, the right to vote, and the right to marry a white person, denied children of Chinese descent access to public schools, denied Chinese immigrants the right to bear arms, unfairly targeted women of Chinese descent by imposing special requirements in order for them to immigrate into the state, authorized the removal of Chinese immigrants to outside town and city limits, denied Chinese laborers employment in public works projects and through state agencies, prohibited the issuance of licenses to Chinese in California, denied Chinese in California the right to fish in California's waters, and unduly taxed Chinese businesses and individuals while denying Chinese laborers; and

Whereas, Chinese in California were denied the right to testify as a witness in any action or proceeding in which a white person was a party, pursuant to a state law which was upheld in People v. Hall (1854) 4 Cal. 399. As a result of the decision to place Chinese in California outside of the protection of the law, many Chinese in California were left extremely vulnerable to violence and abuse; and

Whereas, Chinese in California faced further discrimination under local ordinances which targeted traditional Chinese culture and customs. Laws were enacted forcing Chinese men in San Francisco to cut off their traditional queues, banning the Chinese traditional style of transporting fruits and vegetables, unjustly raising taxes on Chinese-owned laundromats, targeting the Chinese custom of disinterring the remains of their deceased to send back to China for proper burial, and forcing the Chinese in San Francisco to live within an area that was considered unsanitary and unsafe to ordinary individuals. These laws were enacted in order to impose shame and humiliation on Chinese Americans and Chinese immigrants; and

Whereas, California lobbied Congress for years to strictly prohibit immigration from China, and in 1882, was successful in convincing Congress to enact the Chinese Exclusion Act, the first federal law ever passed excluding a group of immigrants solely on the basis of race or nationality. The Chinese Exclusion Act set the precedent for racist foreign and national policy that led to broader exclusion laws and fostered an environment of racism that quickly led to the Jim Crow laws of the 1880s and further segregation legislation that would tear our nation apart through most of the 20th century; and

Whereas, Paradoxically, the very same year that the Chinese Exclusion Act was passed, financing abroad was completed for the Statue of Liberty. The Statue of Liberty is a sign of freedom and democracy and was built and presented to the United States at the same time that Chinese Americans and Chinese immigrants were being denied freedom and democracy. The Statue of Liberty is our nation's great symbol of hope and justice for all who live, and all who wish to live, in the United States of America. While the Statue of Liberty was being built, legislators were contradicting those very ideals by discriminating against Chinese immigrants and lobbying Congress to do the same; and

Whereas, The Chinese Exclusion Act, which originally expired in 1892, was extended by Congress for 10 years in the form of the Geary Act and made permanent in 1902. It remained in effect until it was repealed in 1943 as a result of the alliance forged between China and the United States during World War II. The Chinese were once again allowed to immigrate to the United States, and shortly thereafter California's Angel Island ceased to be used as a detainment center for Chinese immigrants; and

Whereas, Former Article XIX of the California Constitution, which was adopted in 1879 and unfairly targeted and discriminated against Chinese living in California, remained in effect for 73 years until it was repealed in 1952; and

Whereas, Despite decades of systematic, pervasive, and sustained discrimination, Chinese living in California persevered and went on to make significant contributions to the growth and success of our state; and

Whereas, Today, Californians of Chinese descent occupy leading roles in politics, business, and academia. Currently there are 10 Chinese Americans serving in California's constitutional and statewide offices. Jerry Yang, former CEO of Yahoo! Inc., is a California resident. University of California, San Diego, Professor Roger Y. Tsien was awarded the 2008 Nobel Prize in chemistry for his discovery and development of the green fluorescent protein. And this year, California resident Steven Chu, former President of California's Lawrence Livermore National Laboratory and a Nobel Prize winner in Physics, was appointed by President Obama and sworn in as the Secretary of Energy. The contributions of Chinese Americans to the State of California are vast and irreplaceable. They have played a central role in turning California's university system, technology industry, businesses, and agriculture into a world power; now, therefore, be it

Resolved by the Assembly of the State of California, the Senate thereof concurring, That diversity is one of our state's greatest strengths, enabling California to thrive economically, agriculturally, technologically, academically, and politically at an international level. Our great state has relied on immigrants of all backgrounds to build our infrastructure, and integrating them into our society not only helps them prosper, but helps California prosper as well; and be it further

Resolved, That while this nation was founded on the principle that all men are created equal, and while we pay tribute to the great American creed "give me your tired, your poor, your huddled masses yearning to breathe free" which stands at the base of America's Statue of Liberty, a symbol of hope for all who live, and all who wish to live, in the United States of America, we recognize that the practices of our state and its government have not always honored this promise. Ours is a state with an imperfect history where intolerance spurred the enactment of unjust discriminatory laws that have too often denied minority groups access to the promise of America, that all men are created equal. Today that struggle continues, and learning from our past will help enable us to travel further down the path toward building a more perfect Union; and be it further

Resolved, That the Legislature deeply regrets the enactment of past discriminatory laws and constitutional provisions which resulted in the persecution of Chinese living in California, which forced them to live in fear of unjust prosecutions on baseless charges, and which unfairly prevented them from earning a living. The Legislature regrets these acts and reaffirms its commitment to preserving the rights of all people and celebrating the contributions that all immigrants have made to this state and nation; and be it further

Resolved, That the Chief Clerk of the Assembly transmit copies of this resolution to the author for appropriate distribution.

Assembly Concurrent Resolution No. 42
Adopted by the Assembly July 6, 2009

Signed: *Karen Bass*
Honorable Karen Bass
Speaker of the California State Assembly

Attest: *E. Dotson Wilson*
E. Dotson Wilson
Chief Clerk of the Assembly

Signed: *Darrell Steinberg*
Honorable Darrell Steinberg
President pro Tempore of the Senate

Adopted by the Senate July 9, 2009

Attest: *Gregory P. Schmidt*
Greg P. Schmidt
Secretary of the Senate

2009

California Governor Schwarzenegger apologized for the historical Chinese exclusion laws.

Soon after China emerged as a world superpower, the United States and other countries began to apologize for the discriminatory actions against Chinese.

California Governor Arnold Schwarzenegger signed Bill ACR 42 on July 17, 2009 to apologize to the California Chinese for the historical Chinese exclusion laws. The Bill also acknowledges the contribution of Chinese to California, especially the construction of the Pacific Railroad.

2000年以來，中國經濟崛起，成為加州農產品最大的買家。2009年7月17日，加州議會向美籍華人為自19世紀以來所有的歧視法律道歉，由州長史瓦辛格簽署ACR42法案，該法案認可華人對加州的貢獻，特別是太平洋洲際鐵路的修建。

其實早在2006年，加拿大總理哈柏（Stephen Harper）就已向加拿大華人，就19世紀以來的不平等稅收道歉。加州的道歉開啟了第二波道歉潮。

---

59. http://content.time.com/time/nation/article/0,8599,1911981,00.html

Senate Joint Resolution No. 23

CHAPTER 134

Relative to Chinese Americans in California.

[Filed with Secretary of State August 28, 2014.]

LEGISLATIVE COUNSEL'S DIGEST

SJR 23, Huff. Chinese Americans in California.

This measure would acknowledge the history of the Chinese in California, would recognize the contributions made to the State of California by Chinese Americans and Chinese immigrants, and would request Congress to adopt resolutions of apology to the Chinese American community for enactment of the Chinese exclusion laws.

Fiscal Committee: no

WHEREAS, Chinese Americans have a long and rich history in the United States and California; and

WHEREAS, The many contributions of Chinese Americans, both past and present, should be acknowledged and celebrated; and

WHEREAS, Since the late 19th century, Congress enacted adverse laws specifically targeting Chinese people on the basis of race, most notably the Chinese Exclusion Act of 1882; and

WHEREAS, During this period, growth in the Chinese population, combined with economic regression, led to pervasive anti-Chinese sentiments, especially in California and the American West; and

WHEREAS, California's stance against the Chinese community influenced the promotion and passage of the federal Chinese Exclusion Act; and

WHEREAS, California lobbied Congress for years to strictly prohibit immigration from China, and in 1882, was successful in convincing Congress to enact the Chinese Exclusion Act, the first federal law ever passed excluding a group of immigrants solely on the basis of race or nationality. The Chinese Exclusion Act set the precedent for racist foreign and national policy that led to broader exclusion laws and fostered an environment of racism that quickly led to the Jim Crow laws of the 1880s, and further segregation legislation that would tear our nation apart through most of the 20th century; and

WHEREAS, The Chinese Exclusion Act and later amendments to the act not only established barriers exclusively for Chinese attempting to enter the country, it also placed discriminatory restrictions on those already living in the United States, such as requiring Chinese laborers who desired to reenter the country to obtain "certificates of return"; and

WHEREAS, Paradoxically, the very same year that the Chinese Exclusion Act was passed, financing abroad was completed for the Statue of Liberty. The Statue of Liberty is a sign of freedom and democracy and was built and presented to the United States at the same time that Chinese Americans and Chinese immigrants were being denied freedom and democracy. The Statue of Liberty is our nation's great symbol of hope and justice for all who live, and all who wish to live, in the United States of America. While the Statue of Liberty was being built, legislators were contradicting those very ideals by discriminating against Chinese immigrants and lobbying Congress to do the same; and

WHEREAS, Some congressional legislators did warn against the moral bankruptcy of the Chinese Exclusion Act by appealing to America's ideals. Senator George Frisbie Hoar debated against the measure before the United States Senate, stating, "Nothing is more in conflict with the genius of American institutions than legal

2011

The Senate apologized for all the Chinese exclusion laws.

On October 11, 2011, a full Senate apologized for the historical Chinese exclusion laws in the last 129 years.

The SJR-23 (Senate Joint Resolution No. 23) recognizes the contributions made to the State of California by Chinese-Americans and Chinese immigrants, and requests Congress adopt resolutions of an apology to the Chinese-American community for enactment of the Chinese exclusion laws. California Senator Dianne Feinstein said: "I hope the resolution will serve to enlighten those who may not be aware of this regrettable chapter in our history and bring closure to the families whose loved ones lived through this difficult time."

2011年10月11日，美國參議院全數通過為129年來所有的排華法案正式道歉-- SJR-23 (Senate Joint Resolution No. 23)，並確認華人及其他亞洲移民與任何其它國家的移民一樣，都享有同等權利。

本案的發起人是加州民主黨參議員黛安方士丁（Senator Dianne Feinstein），她說：「希望本法案能讓那些不知道美國歷史上有這個令人遺憾的一章的人有所覺悟，也希望那些家人曾經為此而受苦的人因之釋懷」。

---

60. http://latimesblogs.latimes.com/nationnow/2011/10/us-senate-apologizes-for-mistreatment-of- chinese -immigrants.html
61. http://www.1882project.org/

IV

112TH CONGRESS
2D SESSION
H. RES. 683

Expressing the regret of the House of Representatives for the passage of laws that adversely affected the Chinese in the United States, including the Chinese Exclusion Act.

IN THE HOUSE OF REPRESENTATIVES

JUNE 8, 2012

Ms. CHU (for herself, Mr. SMITH of Texas, Mr. HONDA, Mr. ISSA, Mr. BURTON of Indiana, Mr. CLAY, Ms. LEE of California, Mr. GRIJALVA, Mr. SCHIFF, and Mr. JACKSON of Illinois) submitted the following resolution; which was referred to the Committee on the Judiciary

---

RESOLUTION

Expressing the regret of the House of Representatives for the passage of laws that adversely affected the Chinese in the United States, including the Chinese Exclusion Act.

Whereas many Chinese came to the United States in the 19th and 20th centuries, as did people from other countries, in search of the opportunity to create a better life;

Whereas the United States ratified the Burlingame Treaty on October 19, 1868, which permitted the free movement of the Chinese people to, from, and within the United States and made China a "most favored nation";

Whereas in 1878, the House of Representatives passed a resolution requesting that President Rutherford B. Hayes

2012

Congress apologized for the Chinese Exclusion Act.

On June 18, as Bill 282 was passed, a full house in Congress apologized for 130 years of Chinese exclusion laws.

2012年6月18日，在《排華法案》通過後的130年後，美國眾議院終於在第683號議案中，正式對過去所制定的排華法案表示歉意。

---

62. http://www.advancingjustice-la.org/blog/con-ress-soon-pass-apology-chinese-exclusion-act#.V5huLbh97IU

2012

Residents in Riverside California saved Chinatown history.

By 1868, many Chinese were living in Riverside, California. In 1885, after Riverside passed a law forbidding Chinese to run businesses there, Chinese were forced to move out of the city and settle nearby. In 1940, Wang Ho Leung was the sole Chinese resident left in Chinatown. He passed away in 1974 and his property was sold to a developer. The last building in Chinatown was torn down in 1977 and all the historical relics were buried underground. In 1980, the Education Department of Riverside County bought this property and some partial digging discovered significant historical relics. In 2008, Riverside City Council decided to build a medical building on the site, and the "Save our Chinatown Committee" was formed to stop the development. In March 2012, the Appellate Court decided that Riverside Countydid not consider all the reasonable alternatives before it built upon the old Chinatown site. Today, the Riverside residents are looking forward to the first Chinatown Heritage Park which will be built on the old Chinatown site.

1868年，中國人就到了加州的河邊市（Riverside）。1885年，河邊市立法不准中國人經商，他們只好搬出市中心，到附近的地方買房子，最後因為「排華法案」，中國城還是沒落了。1940年，小城剩下最後一位華人居民黃河亮，他於1974年過世，他在中國城的房地產被一家開發公司買下，1980年轉賣給河邊市的教育部門。史學家發現在這塊地底下有許多遺物，對研究美國華人歷史將有極大的貢獻。但教育部門卻在1990年決定在現址建立一所醫學大樓。維護中國城古蹟的人立刻成立「拯救中國城委員會（Save Our Chinatown Committee）」，對河邊市教育部門提告。2012年，法院判決「拯救中國城委員會」勝訴，法官認為摧毀中國城古蹟是不對的。中國城遺址被保留了，現在將在該遺址上建立第一座中國城紀念公園「Riverside Chinatown Heritage Park」。

---

63. http://www.saveourchinatown.org/aboutchinatown.html

ACKNOWLEDGMENTS

The views expressed in this book are mine. However, I could not have completed the work of such magnitude without the help of many people, including those who assisted me in years past with the exhibition of Herstory.

My special gratitude goes to:

Sa-Chou Lu, Professor Kuo-Jung Tsai, Li-Shiang Liu, Wayne Lin, Henry Chen, Wen-Tong Chiu, Wei-Shiang Chen, Kuo-Sheng Hsu, David Lau, Annie Tsai, His Excellency David Lee, Po-Chun Lai, Li-Chuan Tu, Pei-Chun Yang, Mei-Yun Chen, Rinsin Wang, Christine Liang, Echo Tsai, Xien-Shun Wang, Tai-Tien Hong, Philip Choy, Pamela Wong, Angela Chen, Le Le Chen, Renee Philson, Debby Liang, Grace Liang, Tracy Chen, Alva Liang, Grace Yang, Julia Tsai, Sara Fong, Ginny Fang, Christine Jiang, Lily Tong, Allison Tom, Grace Chou, Ted Schulze, the Honorable Lily Lee Chen, Teddy Zee, Kuo-Hua Lee, Ben Wang, Li-Hua Chen, Po-Chuan Chen, Su-Hui Chen, Maggie Chang, Yu Min Weng, Lavinia Chan, Florence Fang and Zoey Weng.

PHOTO CREDITS

Cover: Juwin Liu

P. 10: Library of Congress

P. 12-13: National Palace Museum, Taiwan

P. 14: Records of the United States Supreme Court

P. 16: Wikipedia

P. 18: California State Archives, Wikipedia

P. 20, 22-23: Iowa State Archives

P. 24: Wikipedia

P. 26: New York Times

P. 28: Ted Schulze

P. 30: Records of the Immigration and Naturalization Service

P. 34: Juwin Liu

P. 35: Records of the Immigration and Naturalization Service

P. 36: Juwin Liu

P. 38: racialinjustice.eji.org

P. 40: Academia Historica, Taiwan

P. 44-51: The U.S. Army

P. 52-57: Wang Tony, Tien Lulu, Ji Pei-Xia

P. 58-59: Wikipedia

P. 60-61: Wikipedia

P. 62: Wikipedia

P. 64-65: Wikipedia

P. 68: Mi Chu

P. 70: Wikipedia

P. 72: Wikipedia

P. 74: Lily Lee Chen

P. 76: Wikipedia

P. 78: Florence Fang

P. 82: Chinese Historical Society of America

P. 88-89: Jacob Rekedal, Margie Akin

Made in the USA
San Bernardino, CA
25 July 2018